# Easy Book of Thoughts

## KNOWING HOW TO SEE THE REALITY

Amit Verma

*Dedicated to the human being*

*who never sought a reason to love me!*

*(My mother)*

" You are just a tiny wisp of air (soul)
Carrying a big corpse (body)."

Epictetus – Greek Philosopher

# Contents



## Part 1   Understanding the Thoughts

## Part 2  Learning the Ways to Create Good Thoughts
## (Most of the Time)



## Part 3  Perspective and its Effect on Thoughts

## Part 4 Workbook

# Prologue

This book is for everyone who thinks. Generally, we understand the power of our thoughts very late in our life. If someone could tell us about our ability to alter our life by changing our thoughts, it would be a game changer.

If I have to define it in one line then, it is a book for every young person who is stepping out of college to face the real world on his own.

The first part of the book shows you how we can change the way we see the reality by changing our thoughts.

The second part shows us various practical ways to create good thoughts.

The third part shows how perspective changes our thoughts.

The fourth part is a practical workbook which will help you to think more clearly.

Book is a lens to see the things in a different way.

# Why this book?

I am a doctor.

One day I was sitting in my OPD.

Then he visited me.

I have known him for last 10 years. He has been at the top of his job all the time.

He is a medical representative in a reputed pharma company.

He is around 45 years old. And he has seen it all.

But on that day, something was awfully wrong.

He had a sweaty, anxious speech.

His heart was pounding inside his chest, and he had extreme restlessness. He could not stay still in the hospital chair.

An extreme restlessness.

We call it akathisia.

What went wrong?

I had always seen him calm and composed fighting with the thing's life throws with serene bravery.

All tests were normal.

He settled after a few doses of anti-anxiety medication. But it took three hours.

He then left for his city 250 km away in a car.

His two juniors were with him. They were also dumbfounded to see a giant giveaway in this manner.

'Sales targets!' they murmured when I enquired.

I called him in the evening.

He had slept throughout the journey due to the effects of anti-anxiety medications. He still felt anxiety.

I just told him to relax and take some time off.

That was what he was worried about.

He had got a warning to step up his game from his CEO and after 20 years of service he felt helpless for the first time.

I thought about this for a long time.

A strong and successful person like him crumbles under stress in spite of all his experience.

We expect our children to learn from us. About facing adversities.

But what happens when we crumble?

Then I started to write this book for him.

Or should I say for myself.

I fear a similar breakdown coming to me at some point in the future. Such is the ruggedness of our modern life.

Although there is nothing wrong with breaking down under extreme stress, after all, we are all humans. We carry very soft things inside us. We have others to take care of us.

I wanted to prepare myself for such circumstances.

**A man who has never gone to the brink of devastation suddenly faces it.**

Adversities are inevitable.

But we should have a framework to deal with them.

All that our ancestors have accumulated.

Timeless wisdom.

This helps to tide over the life storms.

This is a book for everyone who is feeling stressed by the pace of his life and the turbulence of our times.

Anyone who breaks down with the first storm that hits his door.

This is a book to revisit in the tough times.

This is a book that we give to a person who is falling apart.

This is a book for a kid who is just stepping out of his house. Who has heard about the world but not faced it.

On his next visit after two months, I handed over a rough draft of this book to him.

He took it with a smile, not aware that it was written for him.

I hope he will like it.

# Preface

*The real thoughts, new and genuine that have been thought in this world, up to this time amount to only a handful.*

> \- Swami Vivekananda, a Great
> Indian thinker

Nothing is absolutely true. No one is original. We are all like worms growing on a heap of wisdom which has accumulated over centuries. Anyone who claims to have copyright to this combined wisdom is mistaken.

What I share here is the wisdom that I have gathered while I revolve on this planet.

There is no absolute truth.

Only perspectives.

Frames of thinking which we find useful.

This book weaves a narrative that can be used at many turns of our life.

It may not be true, but it will certainly give some power to you. It will give you a way to see things. A framework. A little window of order in the inherent chaos and randomness of being.

It is a way to see things.

So, let's begin.

# Part 1

# Understanding the Thoughts

# CHAPTER 1

# What is a Thought?

*"Be not afraid of going slowly; be afraid only of standing still."*

– Chinese Proverb

*"If you realised just how powerful your thoughts are, you would never think a negative thought."*

– Anonymous

Hi there.

Man.

Or a woman.

Whoever is reading it.

A child who has learnt to read on his own.

Or an avid reader who has read hundreds of books.

I am here.

Right here.

It's not surprising that you can't see me.

No one can see me.

I am just a vibration of ether.

I am transient turbulence in the Higgs field.

I come, and then I go.

Unless or until you stick to me and keep me alive.

Thank you for that.

I am a thought.

A human thought.

And I am writing this book.

I have to, as there is no book that I have not written.

I am drenched in the ink and then put on onto pages.

◆ ◆ ◆

I am the source of your knowledge.

Primary source of your knowledge.

I am a thought.

A human thought.

# CHAPTER 2

# The Trap

*"Knowledge speaks, but wisdom listens."*

– Jimi Hendrix

I am a disturbance.

Disturbance in the electric circuits of your brain.

I live in the consciousness where you meet me.

Other times, I rest in the subconscious, ready to appear at most unusual times and in the most dire circumstances.

I am an organised disturbance that comes on the screen of your consciousness so that you become aware of it.

Not only aware but you fuse yourself with me.

Then there is no difference between you and me.

I become you and you follow me like a shadow.

You believe in whatever I show, and that is your biggest weakness.

And you take it as a normal thing because everyone is doing it.

You have been doing it since your childhood days.

But it is not the truth.

It is a trap. You are not me and I am not you.

# CHAPTER 3

# Thinking Brain

*The shortest answer is doing.* "

– Lord Herbert

Well, now let's try to tell you in your language.

In the language you seek. As a story.

Your body is like a car.

You. The real you (soul).

What I call the observer is in the back seat.

You cannot photograph it. You can only imagine it. So, let's imagine it—your actual form.

It's a sphere of light. It is connected to the supreme. The Infinite Intelligence. The eternal source of energy and the consciousness of this universe.

You may call it divine—or even God.

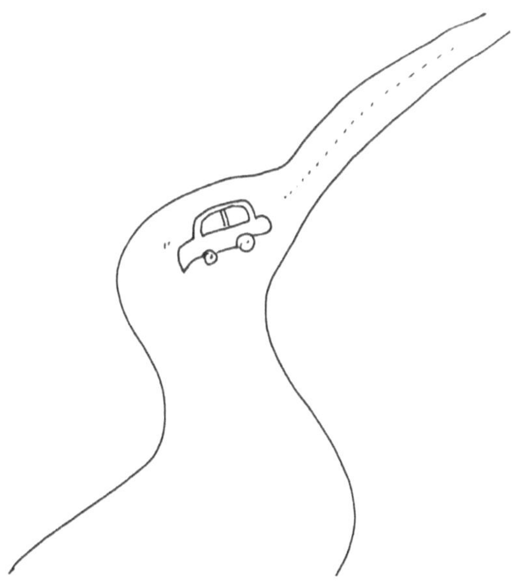

You derive your energy and awareness from it.

You have no limbs.

No mouth.

No weapons.

Just a round sphere of energy.

You cannot stop the thinking brain who is the driver of this car.

You cannot touch it. Or hold it or restrain it.

Why?

Because most of the time you are asleep. Not aware of yourself.

You think you are the driver.

You fuse with it. You think that you are thinking brain.

Let us see the thinking brain now.

The brain is the place of thinking.

It is very naughty.

It is restless. It is incessantly predicting, planning, and analysing.

It doesn't know the difference between a real danger or only a poster on the side of the road.

It presses the accelerator of emotions and brakes of the fear to stop you.

At the slightest danger it puts the brakes on and predicts the doomsday.

On slight doubt, it floods you with painful emotions.

You either burn in anger or fry slowly in the anxieties and worries.

Slowly, you burn out.

# CHAPTER 4

# Two Things to do

*"The road to success is always under construction."*

– Lily Tomlin

Is there any escape?

You can do one thing.

You can observe it. Wake up and watch it.

It takes effort, but it is worth it.

Just stay awake for a sufficient amount of time.

You can see it. Watch how it behaves in different situations. Watch its repetitive behaviours. Things it craves and things it doesn't like.

There is one other thing you can do.

You can see the flow of air inside and outside of the car. That means watch your breathing.

That is more than enough.

By remaining awake, you bring the brain to the present.

It then doesn't drag you to the past where regret, guilt and revenge reside.

It also stops anxieties about the future.

You can do these two things regularly. Then, you can keep the driver under some control.

At least you can keep it in the present.

You will watch it. This will numb it a little. Be the watcher.

# CHAPTER 5

# How to Start!

*"Life is 10% what happens to you and 90% how you react to it."*

\- Charles R. Swindoll

How to start?

You can forgive yourself first.

Your brain is a dumb piece of tissue. It does not know the difference between the real and imaginary dangers.

It doesn't know the difference between the present and the past.

It does not know the difference between good and bad and the amount of a thing required.

It generally overshoots the requirement.

Also, it is addicted to drinking Dopamine (pleasure hormone).

It demands things, and when what it receives overshoots the expectations, it gets a surge of Dopamine. It then craves for more of it.

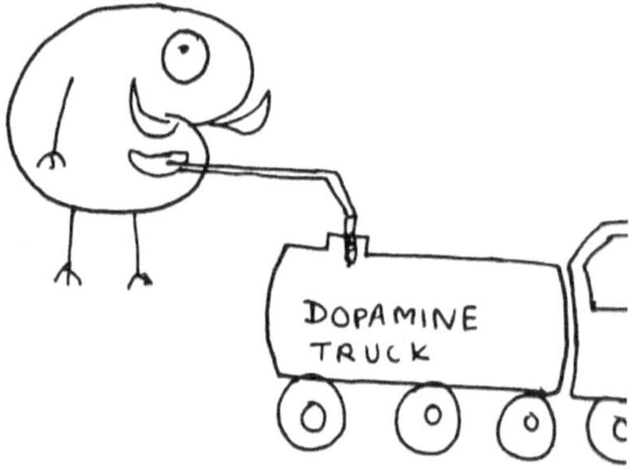


Its unhealthy lifestyle also drenches it into the cortisol (stress hormone), which wears the car slowly.

So forgive yourself for all the mistakes you have made up to now.

It's time for a fresh start.

Know that everyone fails or will fail at some point in time. But those who face life with a sense of responsibility generally prevail.

One other thing is your attitude (windshield of the car). The glass through which you see the world. Your thinking brain also watches through it.

You need to keep it clean. It is the filter through which you see everything. Keep it positive and clean.

So we now know that you can do these things.

1. Forgive yourself for past mistakes.

2. Watch and remain awake.

   (Practice mindfulness)

3. Keep your attitude clean.

# CHAPTER 6

# Breathing

*"Thoughts become things."*

– bob proctor

How to do that exactly?

It's the theoretical part.

Let's get some practical wisdom.

Focus on the air entering the car.

(Your Breathing)

Air comes inside (inspiration).

It goes outside (expiration).

Exhalation should be longer.

Breathing should be intentional.

You should be able to control it when you desire.

You should not become an air-puffing machine in stressful situations.

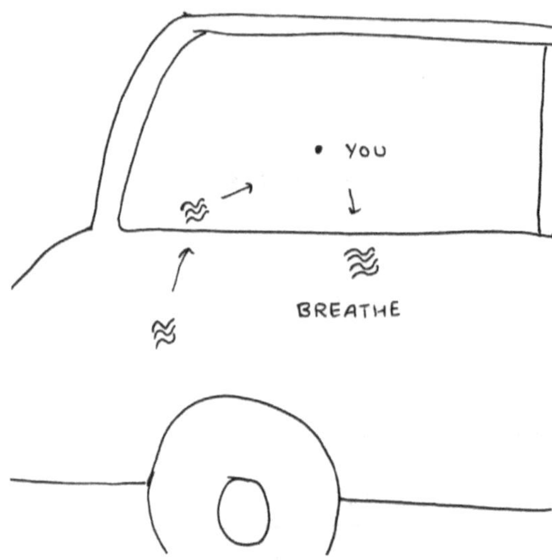


Breathing is a gateway to the present and a valve that controls emotions.

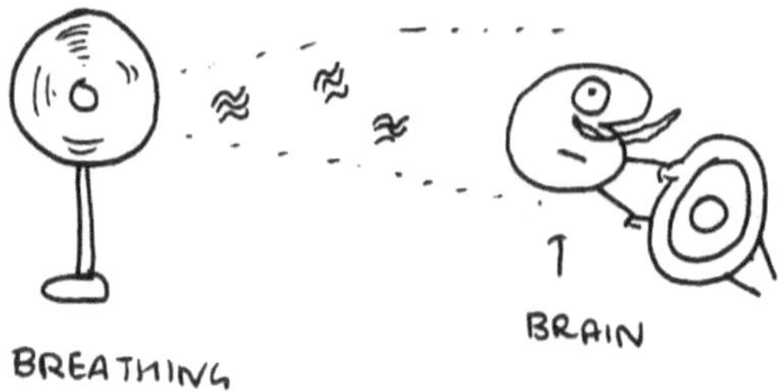


It keeps you awake and healthy.

And it helps you control the flood of emotions that are present randomly.

When you focus on breathing, and you learn to control it, you have your hand on the hand brakes of the car.

You can pull it when things go out of hand.

So, learn to breathe.

Breathe from your nose.

Breathe from the abdomen.

Breathe intentionally.

Try to breathe with voluntary pauses.

# CHAPTER 7

# Things that the Thinking Brain does to Thoughts

*"The key to life is not accumulation.
It's contribution."*

– Stephen Covey

*"If I cannot do great things, I can do small things
in a great way."*

– Martin Luther King Jr.

This driver brain is a weird guy. It takes a thought and distorts it.

This distortion is generally harmful.

Thoughts are neutral.

They are powerless without your response.

But the brain deals with thoughts in the wrong way.

It does these things.

**Personalisation -**

It takes everything personally. An innocent comment becomes an incitement. A gentle smile becomes your mockery. A person sharing his happiness becomes a showoff.

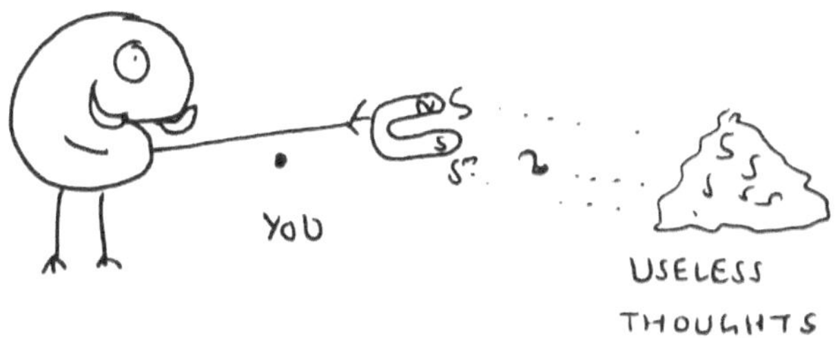


## Generalisation -

It takes one instance and then assumes it to be a universal truth. It creates sheets of fear between you and the world. It punishes everyone in future for the mistake of one person.

**Doomsday scenario -**

It detects a risk and assumes that it will lead to the most disastrous result possible every time. It takes probability as destiny.

**Victim role -**

It puts responsibility for its mistakes on the shoulders of others. Everything going wrong is due to someone's fault.

VICTIMISATION

**Emotional thinking -**

It drenches you in emotions. It sprays them all over so that thinking becomes clouded and erroneous.

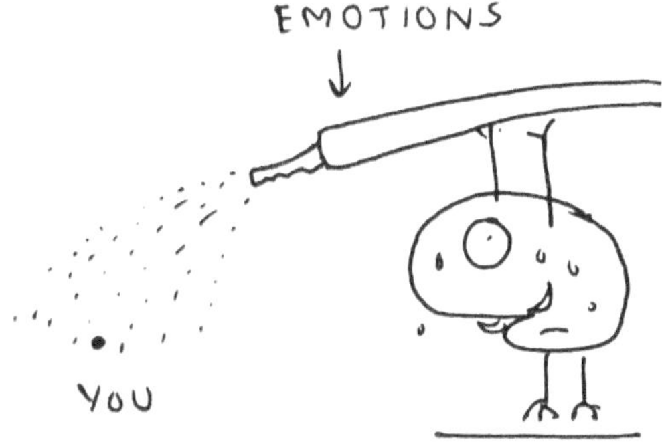



## Mind reading -

It assumes that it can read the minds of others from their actions. Generally, this judgement is wrong.

## All or no thinking -

It thinks in terms of zero or one. In the real world, there is a whole range of possible outcomes. All outcomes are not good or bad.

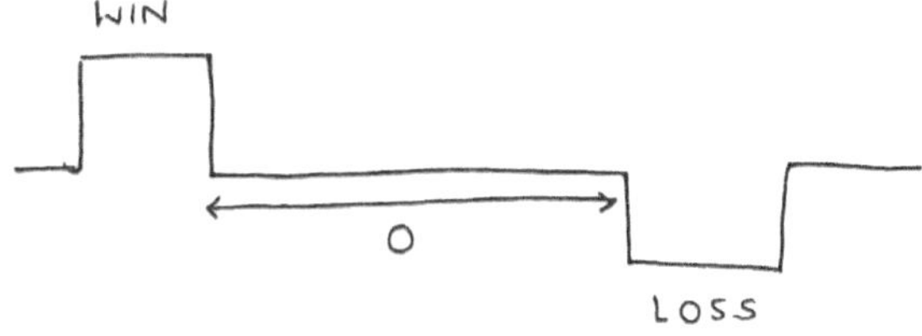

**Fairness illusion -**

It believes in a moral tale that good things will happen to good people. The universe is fair. But that's not always true. The universe is neutral.

So, a pure, innocent thought becomes a monster.

It then throws buckets of stress hormones in the car. You are sleeping but still suffering due to it.

Your body (car) wears down due to this chronic stress. And you, the centre of consciousness, suffer with the brain that has driven you on the wrong path.

So try to see these distortions.

Be the watcher.

Step back frequently and watch your thinking brain.

And take responsibility for your path.

When you put the blame on outside forces, you give away your power.

Keep an internal focus and take responsibility for your life.

# CHAPTER **8**

# Correct Guide

*"The best way out is always through."*

– Robert Frost

*"Be very careful about what you think. Your thoughts run your life."*

– Anonymous

External guides for your car are useful but not perfect.

Praise.

Reward.

Fame.

Riches.

These can pull you but slowly lose effectiveness. You have a natural existence. Any deviation from it will pull you towards your baseline.

Keep an internal drive. An internal compass. It guides your car continuously in the right direction.

Like

justice

Conscience

Courage

Freedom

Peace

Joy.

After you have created an internal guide, align your path with it. Follow your values. These are like GPS to take you to your destination.

Wrong guides can take you on the wrong path. Return from which might be impossible. Don't let your brain, which is a survival machine, guide your life.

This process cuts out most of the contraventions and conflicts from your mind.

Now it's a great feeling.

1.  You know who you are.

2.  Your relationship with your body.

3.  What your brain is doing.

4.  Where it is situated (separate from you)

5.  And those thoughts are benign till you fuse with them.

They are disturbances which need your response to make them effective.

It is the way you interpret them that decides your fate.

And the way you see the external world is decided by the attitude you develop.

What are the things which are under your control?

1.  You watch the thoughts. (Your brain)

2.  You watch the road. (World around you)

3.  You watch yourself. (Metacognition)

4.  You watch your breath. (Gateway to present)

5.  You watch your emotions. (Signals from the body)

You are the watcher.

Always remember that.

# CHAPTER 9

# Emotions

*"A lot of the pain that we are dealing with are really only thoughts."*

You now need to watch emotions.

What are emotions?

These are physical responses of the body to your thoughts.

They drown you frequently.

These are guesses.

These are not facts.

They indicate the current state of your mind and body and their alignment with each other.

They show that you are still fused with your brain.

You need to control your emotions so that you can watch your brain and the road clearly.

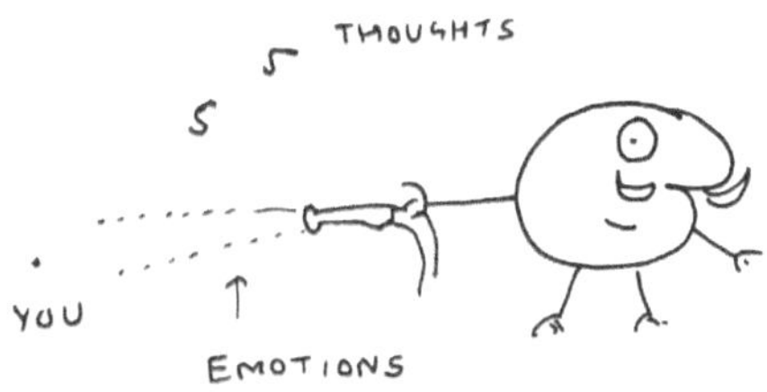

Like thoughts, emotions are powerless until you respond to them in a wrong way.

Emotions are neutral.

They are processes.

Your response to them defines their effects.

You label them.

You give power to them.

You energise them.

They follow a path. They arise and reach a peak and then slowly subside.

You need to give them space and time.

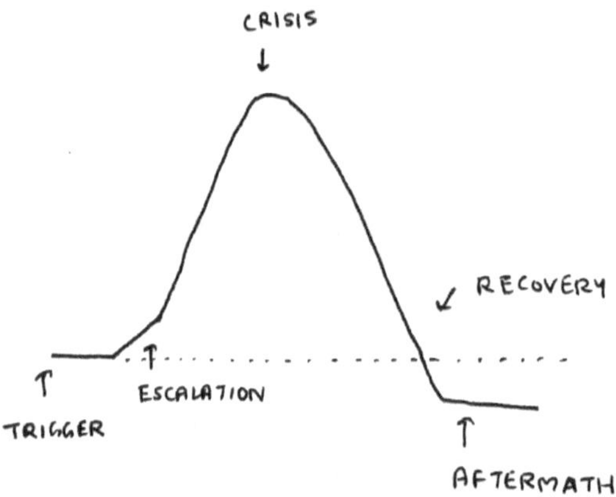



Emotions are positive or negative based on their effects on you and your car or on the society outside.

Although an excess of every emotion is unhealthy.

Let's see what are different types of emotions.

Fear, shame and guilt.

Anxiety and stress

Joy and compassion

Surprise

Anger and Disgust

Sadness and anhedonia

They can be mild (sprinkles or buckets) or enormous (flood)

Emotions are questions. Guess. Indicators of the general state of your body and mind.

Know them that they are not hard and permanent.

That is not always true.

Fleeting phenomena.

Will go away.

If you let them have enough space and time.

What are the things that can help?

See them. Label them. Know that they are signals, not facts.

Don't say," I am sad." Instead, say," I have feelings of sadness at present."

Know that you have a problem.

You are not the problem.

Let them follow their process.

Don't suppress them or avoid them.

In the meantime, you can try some relaxation or soothing techniques.

It can be a hobby or a kind word from your friend.

# CHAPTER 10

# An Emotion called Fear

*"If you want to conquer fear, then go out and get busy."*

– Dale Carnegie

Fear is a universal emotion.

It exists in the background continuously.

Fear has many layers.

When we start to peel its layers, then we encounter many layers.

First is the most superficial cause of fear, like fear of terrorists, fear of flying, fear of public speaking, etc.

Then, if we try to go a little bit deeper, then we find a few common themes that cause all superficial fears.

Various basic causes of fear are.

Loss of reputation

Failure

Rejection

Success

Social isolation

Conflict

Then, if we keep going deeper, we find the basic 'Why' of all your fears.

**It is the feeling of inadequateness.**

If you feel that you might not be able to handle a situation or challenge, then you develop one of these fears.

And then this emotion guides your whole life.

Then, when you act from the mindset of fear, you start to create protective walls around you.

Walls of your mental limitations.

These then keep you mediocre.

Apart from that, these will haunt you whenever you look back at your life.

**How to face fear, then?**

Reset your thinking.

Change your relationship with your thinking brain.

One way is avoidance. You start to avoid situations that create fear. But it is not the right way. You walk through life like you have a thorn stuck in your heel. You protect that thorn from everything and everyone.

You feel the fear frequently, and you reach nowhere.

The second way is active management.

You feel the fear but act in spite of it. This creates opportunities. It creates growth. It strengthens you. It gives you power.

Know that fear will always be there. You can never eliminate it. But act in spite of fear and know that it will make you stronger.

The feeling that you get when you act in spite of your fear is very close to the feeling of exhilaration.

Action cures the fear. Successful people have fears but they act in spite of these.

One good technique is to consider yourself a winner when you take the first step to do a thing that you fear. Don't bother about the results. This will increase your self confidence. When you gain confidence in one area of life then it spills over to other aspects of life too. This makes you even better. This will also shift your focus from outcome to the process. You can control the process but you cannot control every outcome.

These practices can be learnt by anyone.

When you don't attach to your emotions, it makes them weak. Let the comment or emotion that you fear pass through you. Don't react to it or cling to it.

Let it pass.

Know that you have to either accept it or respond to it.

Don't create a problem from it that feeds your ego, which needs to play the victim.

# CHAPTER 11

# Other Emotions

*"The happiness of your life depends upon the quality of your thoughts."*

– Marcus Aurelius

Now, after we have worked on our main emotions, let's see other emotions.

What can you do with unpleasant emotions?

You have many options.

You can avoid them. (Not good)

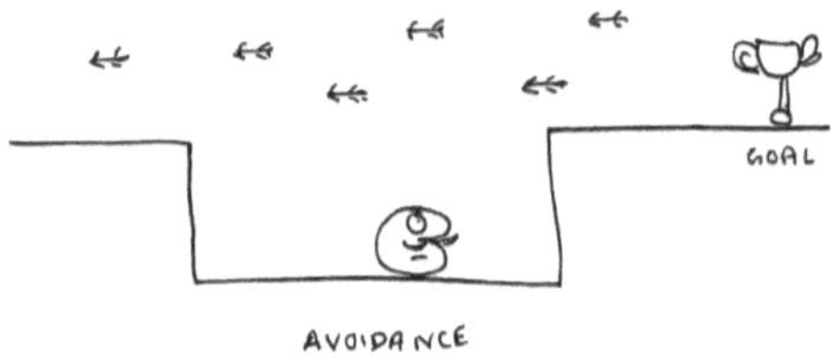


Alter them into challenge or excitement. (Better)

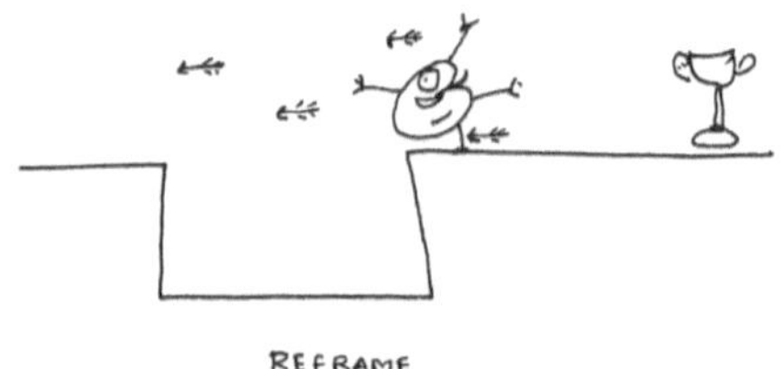

Accept and face gracefully. (Best)

Label your emotions. Own them. Give them some space for the time till they dissipate. Don't stick to them. Let them be. Don't energise them.

Adapt with time. (Meditation)

But do not suppress them.

Putting sand over them will not drown them.

Create distance from them.

Watch them. Go back to your watcher seat.

Know that you are not emotions, but you are having emotions.

Or we can say in reality, you are thinking about emotions and, hence feeling them.

Label them so that you can know exactly what they are here for. See the story behind them.

Avoid ruminating. Negative emotions attract more negative emotions. Don't create a hump of negative hay in your life.

Welcome them.

Avoid two arrows.

One arrow is emotion.

Second is your exaggerated response.

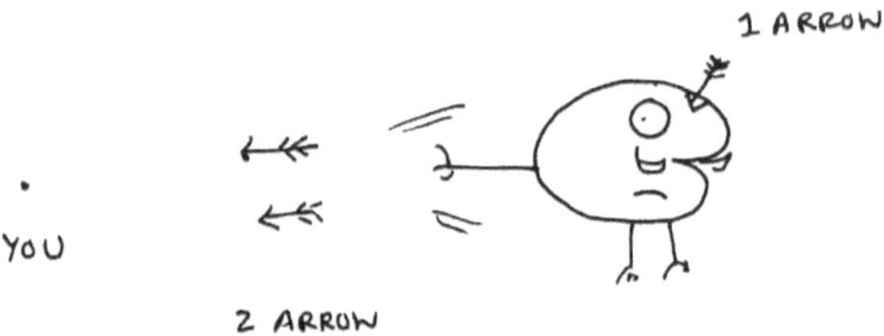


Let them follow their course.

Accept. Be curious.

Observe.

Breathe.

**Sedona method of letting bad emotions go –**

This is a method to deal with bad emotions. This is a five step process.

First – Welcome the emotion. Be aware of it. Notice what it signals. Give it some space to be here.

Second ask this question – "Could I let go this emotion?"

Third ask – "Would I let go this emotion?"

Then ask – "When will I let it go?"

And repeat this process to deal with all unpleasant emotions.

This technique was discovered by Hale Dwoskin.

Let them pass.

BE THE WATCHER

Face the negative emotions with bravery and resolve.

Do some rituals. Some soothing rituals.

Breathing will help.

Relaxation exercises will help. These bring you to the present. These calm your nerves. Breathing controls everything inside the car.

Various things that can help us can be grouped under following categories –

**Immediate things** –

These work for short term. Distract yourself or interrupt the emotion. Distraction can be listening to music or reading or doing some other task. Distraction should not be harmful in itself. Munching on fries and binge watching TV are not the best ways to distract yourself.

You can remember **RAIN** method.

R - Recognise the unpleasant emotion.

A - Allow it to be.

I - Investigate and analyse it.

N - Nurture yourself through self- compassion.

Or you can remember **HALT** method.

Whenever you have to make an important choice or you feel that you are losing to your bad impulses, ask yourself few questions.

Ask if you are hungry, angry, lonely or tired.

If answers are yes, then delay your decision. Come back to it after you have fixed these things.

Do it anyway or at least do something about it. Any small step will help.

Write it down and discuss with someone.

Let go bad emotions using Sedona method, which is described in the last section.

Use relaxation techniques described below.

**Long-term solutions –**

Journal about your emotions. Analyse the root cause of recurrent emotional patterns.

Exercise. Do meditation. Sleep better.

Create good habits and rituals.

If everything does not work get professional help.

Below are a few relaxation techniques that can be helpful.

**Square window technique -**

It is a way to slow down your breathing.

Watch any window or square things like painting around you.

Breathe in for 4 seconds.

Hold your breath for 4 seconds.

Exhale for over 4 seconds.

See your panic wither away.

As you breathe slower, your mind calms down.

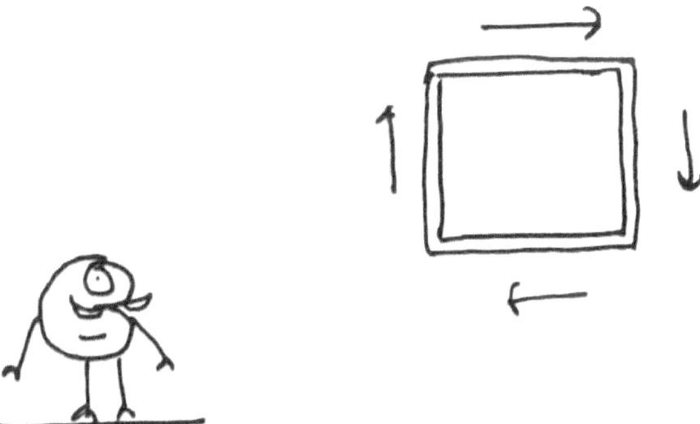

## Counting -

It also brings you in control of your brain. Count till you calm down. Count slowly.

## Grounding by using senses –

It is especially useful in extreme anxiety and panic attacks. It brings you back to the present moment. Observe your surroundings.

First, find 5 things around you that you can see.

Next, find 4 things around you which you can touch.

Next, notice 3 things that you can hear.

Then find two things that you can smell.

And finally, find one thing that you can eat.

This is also called 5-4-3-2-1 technique.

During this time generally you regain some calmness.

## Belly breathing -

It creates intentional deep breathing.

## Correct way to breathe

As you humans evolved your jaws became smaller and your organ of breathing (larynx) shifted downwards in your neck. Due to this you became more prone to chocking and along with that you started breathing in a wrong way.

So you need to learn how to take air into your lungs in a healthy way. Breathing is the main switch to change direction of your thoughts, emotions and nervous system.

Breathe from your nose. Breathing from mouth is harmful for your health.

Breathe slowly. Inhale fully and exhale fully.

Expel the air out of your lungs completely.

A good method can be inhalation for 5 seconds and exhaling for 5 seconds. Practice it during your breaks to make it a frequent habit. It is a good exercise for your lungs. It trains you to breathe slowly when put under stress.

Along with this you need to put your lungs under some stress intermittently. This can be done by ancient breathing techniques described in ancient books. These require practice and patience.

Few techniques which might help you are given below. These are to be learnt from teachers and then practiced.

Pranayama are types of ancient yogic breathing techniques. You can learn them to reap great benefits.

Here are few main types of pranayama techniques.

**Nadi Shodhan kriya** – It is a breathing technique in which you inhale from one nose, hold the breath and then exhale from other nose.

**Bhastrika pranayama** – In this we fill our lungs vigorously and then expel air with force. Both inhalations and exhalations are forceful.

**Sheetkari pranayama** – It cools the body. Inhale with slightly open lips and teeth. Hold the breath and then expel through nose.

**Kapalbhati pranayama** – In this method we use abdominal muscles to exhale forcefully. When abdomen relaxes then lungs are filled with air passively.

Other breathing techniques

**5.5 breathing technique** – Inhale for 5.5 seconds and exhale for 5.5 seconds. It is a way to learn voluntarily to control your breathing.

**Sudarshan kriya** – It involves various steps including mantra chanting. It is an advanced form of rhythmic and cyclical breathing exercise. It involves putting your hands on different parts of front of your trunk and practicing slow and deep breathing.

You inhale while you count from 1 to 4.

Then you hold the breath as you count from 1 to 4.

Then you exhale as you count 1 to 6.

After doing this for significant time, you do deep breathing pranayama (bhartsika pranayama) for 30 to 50 times.

Then you repeat it three times. It is done for 30 to 45 minutes.

It requires patience and dedication. You should search for it, if you want to learn it or you need to join a meditation retreat or course.

**Other things which help to calm the unpleasant emotions.**

BREATHE

Channel them as excitement or challenge.

Reframe the situation.

Attach it to some higher goal if you have a strong 'Why'; you can bear almost anything.

If you think of your work as a medium to improve this world, fear stays a little away.

Know that it will subside.

Know that everyone feels it. Know that stress is part of your survival kit. It puts you in peak performance. Ready to fight.

BREATHE

A little stress is necessary for a meaningful life.

Write your stressful thoughts into your diary.

Journaling means taking down your thoughts on paper. It brings the thoughts to face to face in physical form. You can see them as such. It brings down the veils.

It is like clicking a photo of your thoughts and watching them like an old spy.

You can also plan possible solutions in your diary.

You can put a full stop to an open loop.

Closing the loop calms your brain. Scientists call it the **Zeilgarnick effect.**

It's like showing your brain in written form what it is thinking as such.

It shows reality to the brain.

It can reveal distortions of thought and emotions.

Level of emotions.

The futility of repeating.

And the possible solutions.

Separate your worries and negative emotions into two heaps.

If it is a thing you can't control, let it go. Surrender to it and accept it. Start afresh.

And if you can do something, act with a positive intent without worrying about the results.

Respond, don't react.

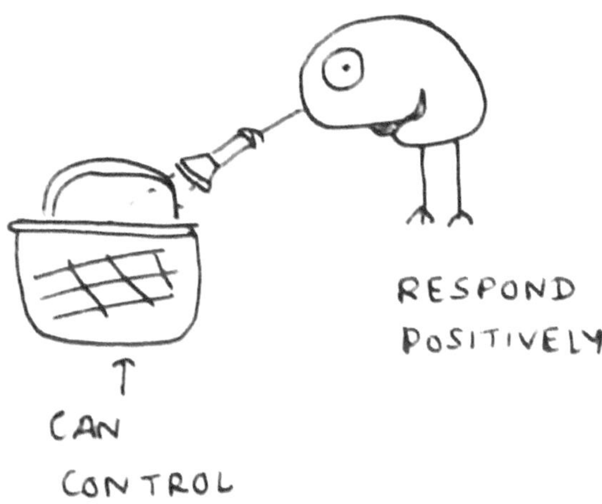


Focus on these things.

1. What you can control.

2. What you can do.

3. What you have.

4. Remain in the present.

5. What is your ultimate purpose?

Then, give a good response.

Try to learn to respond.

Not to react.

## In brief, these are things we can do to handle worry.

Don't hide it. Don't ignore it. Face the worry. Break it down into its components. Write it down. See what you can control. Then, respond positively. Let go of the rest.

You cannot control everything.

Don't forget you are revolving on a rotating stone placed in a huge void. Let the universe decide the things you cannot control. For everything else, give a logical best response and have faith.

# CHAPTER 12

# Other Tricks that you can try to Control your Anxiety/Stress.

*Don't let yesterday take up too much of today.*

— Will rogers

**Baby**

See anxious thoughts like a baby who is crying at 3 am. You have trouble getting up, but you need to settle the baby before you can sleep. Take it in your hands. Don't push it below the cover. Watch it go to sleep slowly.

CRYING BABY

**Wise man**

See these thoughts as a wise person who has come to teach you some important lesson. Get into a student mindset.

Learn what you can learn so that you will not repeat it. Keep the lessons in your mind.

## Sky

See yourself as sky and emotions as thunder and rain. They can't harm you permanently. As the weather clears, it will be great again.

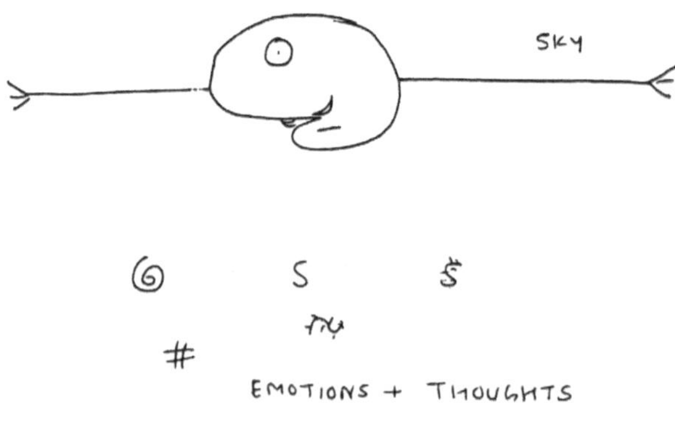

## Dress

See your emotions as you dress for the moment. If it doesn't look good, change it after some time.

## Declutter

Clean your room and reduce stimulation like screens and sounds. This calms your nerves.

Soothing scents help to calm the nerves. Make a corner in your house your relaxation retreat. Go there to recharge and heal. It can be your garden or your library. Engage in your hobbies.

## Share

Share bad emotions and good emotions with close friends and family.

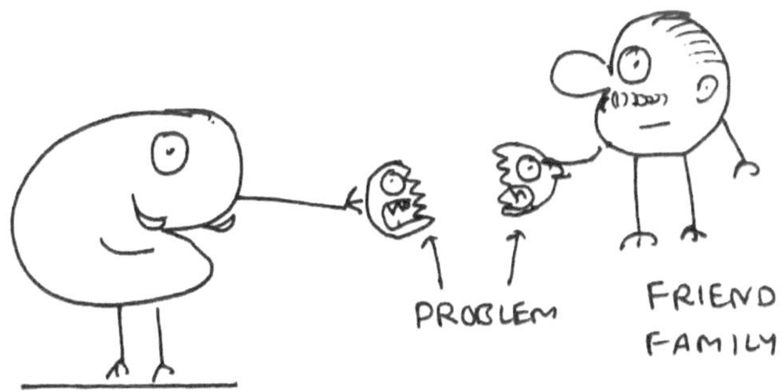


Seek solace. Sharing halves, the pain.

Sometimes, all you need is somebody saying that it will be better tomorrow.

## Give help

Helping others in tough times makes you calmer. Give your presence to a suffering person. You don't have to say anything. You don't have to do anything. Just be there. If possible, listen to him. Let him drain himself.

Be there.

Tell them that you know that your friend is suffering.

Ask what you can do.

Listen compassionately.

Kind words.

Tell him that it is temporary.

## So far, so good.

You know the truth.

You know how to watch thoughts.

You know how to watch and control emotions.

What is next?

# CHAPTER 13

# Two Lifelines

Two ways to get back your power from your thinking brain

1. **Don't play the victim -**

   Do not blame external events for your problems. Know that you have all the resources to pull yourself out of all the problems. Playing victim will mean that you will have to wait for someone else to improve your condition. This is a helpless situation. Don't play a victim. Take responsibility for your life.

2. **Don't complain -**

   When you complain, then you create more problems and disputes. In place of that, focus on the solutions. Complaining never solves anything. If someone has committed a mistake, communicate once with a possible solution. After that, start your work on solving the problem.

## Few Other Sigma Techniques to Face Adversity.

1. See yourself as the **sea**. Your surface is full of movement and full of chaos. But deep down, there is stillness and calm. Whenever you feel restlessness, imagine yourself going into the depths of your stillness.

2. Be **transparent** to hard words. Imagine that accusations and names they call you or complaints you get from them are like air. Weightless and invisible. Be transparent like glass. Let them pass through you. Don't hold onto them or energise them. Let them fade away with time.

3. When you cannot change the situation or pain has crossed your tolerance limits, then **surrender**. All pain is due to resistance. Surrender. It doesn't mean to resign from it. Accept it. Stop creating more pain. Clear your conscience and act from a position of positive intent. Acceptance takes away power from the thinking brain and ego and opens new doors.

4. Try to **match** your expectations with reality outside and your vision inside. This creates less friction. This means making an effort to choose a job, lifestyle, and partner that aligns with your personality and expectations and vice versa. Don't chase every shining thing.

See yourself as the deep sea.

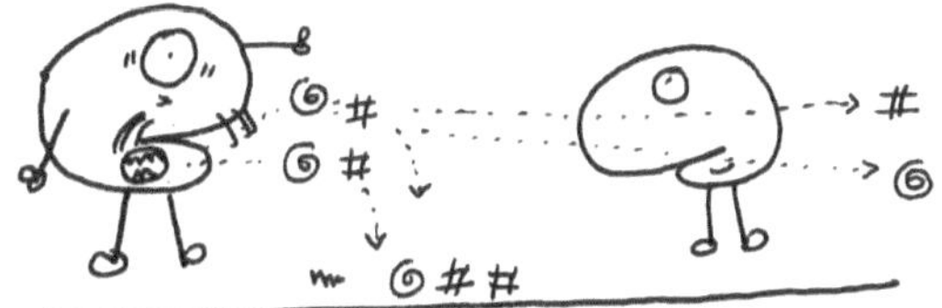

Be transparent to negative influences.

Surrender if you have no control.

Align inner and outer worlds.

# CHAPTER 14

# Two Firewalls for Life

*"Every man dies. Not every man lives."*

– William Wallace

Other two things you can do to bring more joy to your life are

1. **Gratitude -**

   Say, thank you to the universe for all the good things. Everyday. Without fail. So, that infinite intelligence keeps your light bright and your senses sharp. It keeps your windshield clean. Your car is healthy and full of fuel. Full of hope. Running calmly on the timeline of the universe.

   You can do following things. At bedtime remember three good things that have happened that day. Remember three blessings that you have in your life.

   Write these in your dairy. Reflect on your blessings and thank the universe for these.

Gratitude is closely related to the philosophy of **stoicism.**

Stoics advocate living a life of poise and tranquillity.

Stoics advocate following mindsets to live a good life.

1. Imagine the worst thing that can happen to you and thus appreciate all the blessings you have. **(Negative visualisation)**

2. Voluntarily feeling discomfort as a mild vaccine **(hormesis)** to prepare yourselves for bigger

problems. Like fasts, cold showers, and doing things that you fear.

3. An approach of **fatalism** against the past. Whatever happened was destined to happen, and it cannot be changed now. Better to be optimistic about the future.

4. When faced with challenges, find things you can control or at least partially control. Accept other things. This is called **trichotomy of control.**

5. **Forgiveness -**

Know that you forgive somebody for yourself.

Not for anyone else.

Forgive honestly.

Unconditionally.

For yourself.

Stop burning in the heat of the anger. Forgive and feel that the air you are bathed in turns cosy and cold.

Forgive everyone.

**Yourself.**

**Your brain.**

**Your pain.**

**Your mistakes.**

**Your failures.**

**Universe.**

**Forgive and let go.**

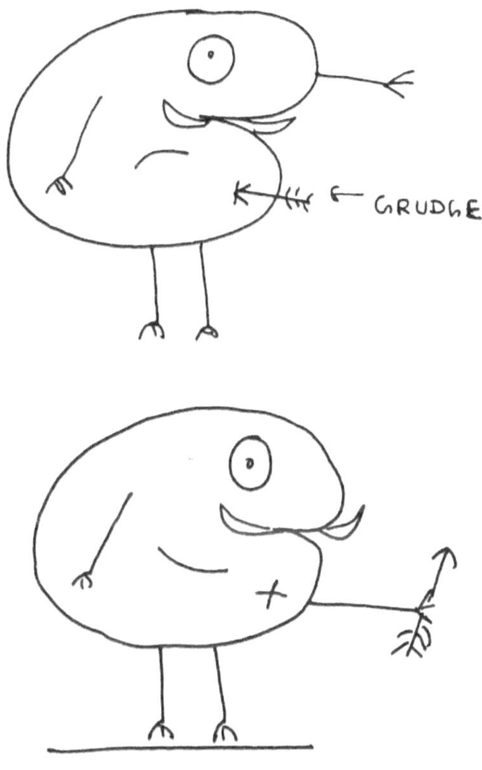

# How to Forgive

1. See all the benefits of forgiving, like peace and lightness.

2. Decide that you want to forgive the person.

3. Know you have a choice, and you can choose forgiveness.

4. See the action from the perspective of that person. See circumstances which forced him or her to do the act which hurt you.

5. See your contribution to the process, which might be very small but still relevant.

6. Forgive the person and let the grudge go. It's the most difficult part. Take your time.

7. Know that this will not change that person, but it will improve your life.

8. Practice self-compassion. Know that you are choosing happiness.

9. Remember when somebody else had forgiven you.

10. Keep trying till you succeed.

After you have done that, you will feel that the car is suddenly faster, lighter, and happier. It's like a flying aeroplane.

## How can you do all that?

We have learnt many things which can help us. These are not all easy. These are all learnable. Try to control your thinking brain using all these techniques.

It's by practice.

Observe.

Without judging.

Daily.

Focus on breathing.

Or sit quietly.

Watch your brain.

Learn Zen

Learn meditation.

Learn mindfulness.

Sit quietly.

In solitude.

Slowly but surely, you will learn to control the brain so that you move with purpose in your life.

# CHAPTER 15

# Taming the Mind

*"We need much less than we think we need."*

– Maya Angelou

Meditation and mindfulness

Now, when you have gained a bit of control over your car, mind, and emotions.

And you have forgiven everyone, including yourself, and thanked the infinite intelligence. (Gratitude)

Let's now see the technique of meditation that strengthens you.

## Simple Method to Learn Meditation

Meditation is an effortless focus on the infinite. It is not sitting alone. It is not simply trying to push away the thoughts. It is not a fixed technique. There are infinite ways to do meditation, but the final destination remains the same. To free yourself from your thinking brain.

## Purpose of meditation

5% of the purpose is served by the object of the meditation. It should be a good object. If you wish to achieve selfish ends through meditation, the whole process fails.

95% is by your attitude while doing meditation. Pursue selfless, noble goals.

The filter through which you see reality is called attitude.

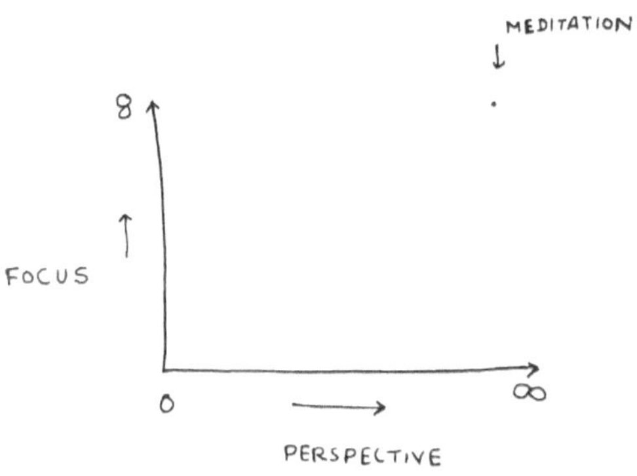


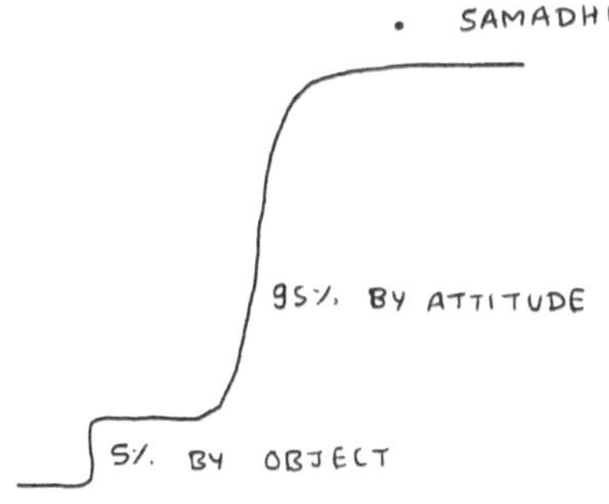

Any posture is good.

Any time is good.

Any place is good.

## Essential parts of mindfulness –

No judgment about the events or thoughts.

Accept the thoughts as they are.

Observe thoughts and emotions.

Stay in the present moment.

## Basic requirements

Abstain from worldly desires.

Reduce stimulation.

Avoid indulgence in short-lasting pleasures.

Stop fixing your happiness on something outside your car. That is insane. There is nothing outside to guide you.

Turn inwards for the correct path.

**Stages of meditation for you according to Patanjali yoga.**

Meditation is the way to move towards infinite intelligence.

There is no path outside.

There is no fixed technique for it.

Only hints about good practices.

**Stages of meditation**

According to the great sage Patanjali, there are eight limbs of yoga that can be used to unite the mind with infinite intelligence.

Types of yoga practices that can be used to achieve divinity are -

1. Karma yoga - Achieving divinity through work.

2. Bhakti yoga - Achieving divinity through devotion.

3. Raj Yoga - Achieving divinity by controlling the mind.

4. Jnana yoga - Achieving divinity through knowledge.

Eight parts or stages of Patanjali yoga/meditation -

1. Yama - Restraint on senses and moral discipline

2. Niyama - Healthy routines

3. Asana - Good posture

4. Pranayama - Controlling breathing

5. Pratyahara - Turning inwards

6. Dharna - Concentration

7. Dhyana - Meditation

8. Samadhi - Return to the source

Follow disciplines and processes of life.

Attain a good and comfortable posture

Lotus or hero or any conformable posture.

Focus on your breathing

BREATHE

Withdraw from outside sensations.

Concentrate on your thoughts.

CONCENTRATION

Watch your thoughts mindfully. Don't make any effort. Let them appear in your consciousness and then move around and finally vanish with a plop.

Your ultimate goal is to attain samadhi, which means the original and eternal state.

And then increase its time.

Go deeper. As the depth of meditation increases, you feel more and more bliss.

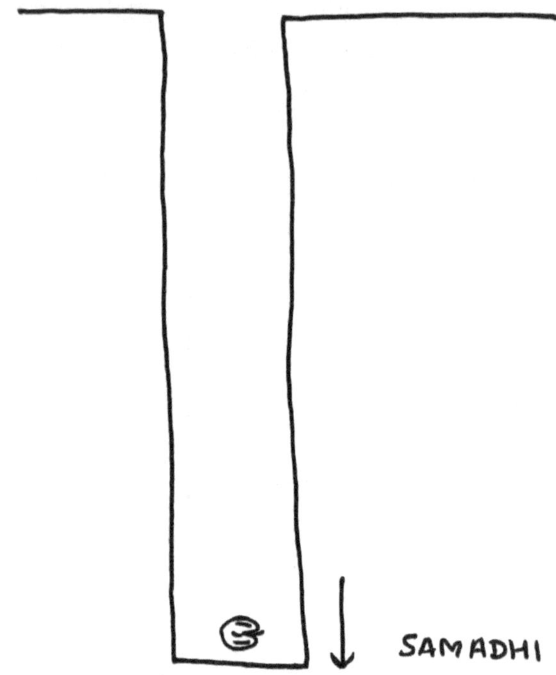


It will make you the master of your brain and body.

All these things will help you to control your car so that it stays on a meaningful and peaceful path.

# CHAPTER 16

# Meaning

*"There is no way to happiness – happiness
is the way."*

– Thich Nhat Hanh

Now comes the question.

**Meaning of it all?**

Where is this car going?

Oh. It is a difficult question that a whole generation of philosophers have tried to answer.

Why are you here after all?

Sitting inside a car (body) driven by your brain. Marching on an unknown path.

Running over a spinning ball of silica and metals.

Let's look back on our life.

It started a long time ago.

You don't remember.

You were asleep.

Infinite intelligence awakened you in the womb of your mother.

Or even before that. Nobody knows. Our consciousness doesn't exist there.

Then came the consciousness. When exactly did it appear; we don't know.

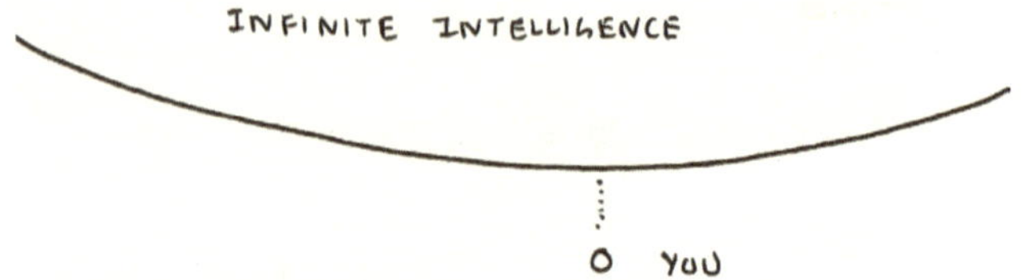


You were full of energy and light. Your brain was purest. It was empty.

You opened your eyes, and everything was new. Unknown.



Your parents drove you both: you and the thinking brain.

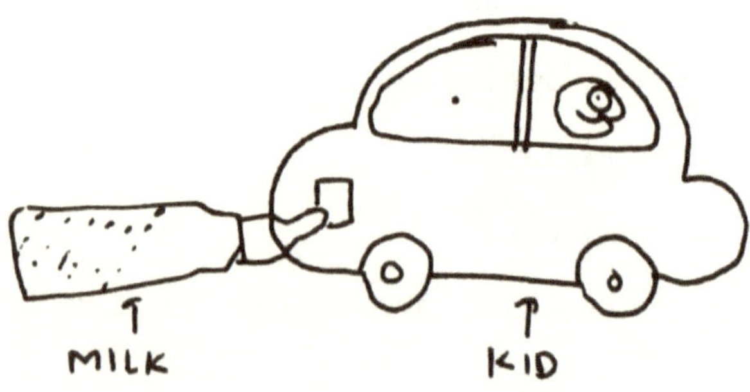

But your brain was very small and unable to create thoughts and emotions.

But slowly, it learned it all.

By watching your mother and father and everyone who was taking care of you.

You don't remember when exactly you fused with your brain.

You were pure. Then, you became an imitation machine. Your thinking brain grows stronger with external conditioning. You slowly forgot that you were separate.

It carried you everywhere.

Your seat on the back of the car remained vacant. Or you kept sleeping there.

For too long.

Intelligence was always there, but it was asleep. Or dormant.

You put a big 'I' on your car and started to drive it around. This 'I' is your ego or Identity.

You called yourself a son.

A student.

A topper.

A brother.

A forward footballer.

A skater.

A college student.

You grew with time.

Your mind is changed by consuming thoughts from outside.

You didn't change. It's the same sphere of energy.

But you never looked inside.

You never thought like that.

The thing that you are not your brain.

Nobody told you.

As you can see, what you are thinking means you are separate from the thinking part.

You can step back and see the thinking part (your brain).

**We call it metacognition.**

It shows that you are not your thoughts.

You are not your brain. Everything changes with time, but you remain the same.

You are the watcher.

The part of consciousness that can see thoughts as well as analyse them.

So, you developed an ego.

Myness.

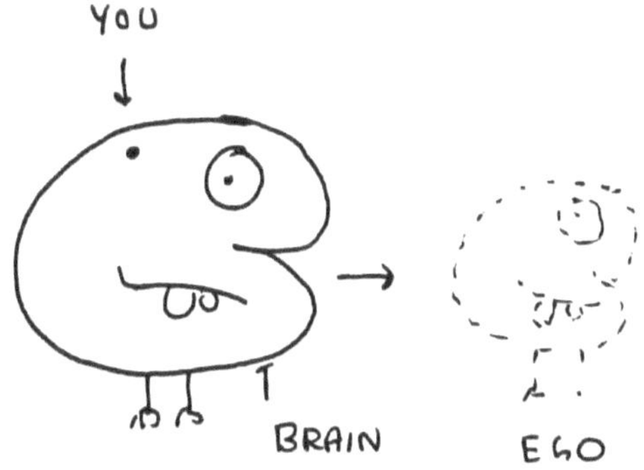

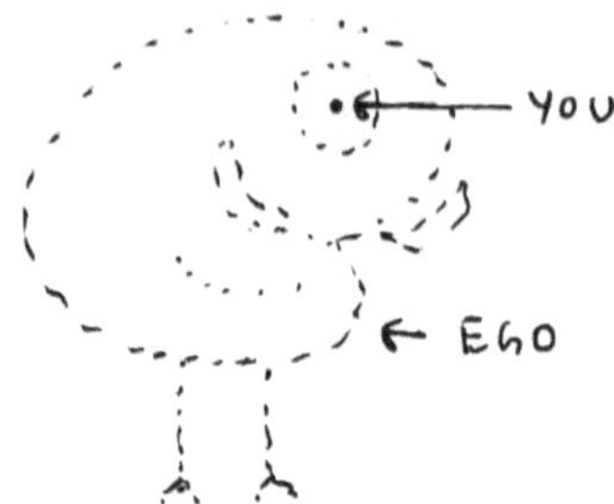


Which is not a bad thing. It keeps you separate and independent to carry out your purpose here.

It is an identity. It is like an identity card you carry around your neck for yourself and others you see.

The problem is when you start to believe that you are that identity card.

The ego tends to develop many bad traits.

Entitlement.

Envy.

Lust.

Greed.

Public pleasing.

Desperation.

Fear.

Hopelessness.

Anxiety.

Self-sabotage.

Nihilism.

# CHAPTER 17

# Awakening

*"It is hard to beat a person who never gives up."*

– Babe Ruth

But at every point, you forget that you are separate from your brain.

The brain is just a tool.

A prediction machine.

It keeps you safe and helps you multiply.

This is its job.

But it is not you.

It is not the master.

It is not the leader.

It is not the one who survives the death.

You are eternal energy. The physical forms are temporary.

You are in the backseat.

Sleeping.

Dormant.

Half awake.

Like a small hair on a big whale.

Moving with it.

**Till something awakens you again.**

It can be many things.

An extreme tragedy.

Failure.

Loss.

Extreme beauty.

Solitude.

A book.

Adventure.

A mentor.

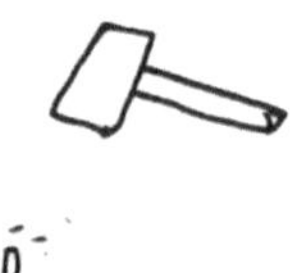

AWAKENING

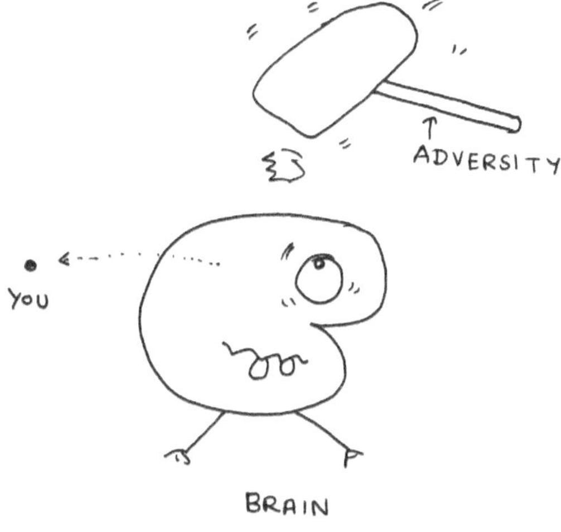


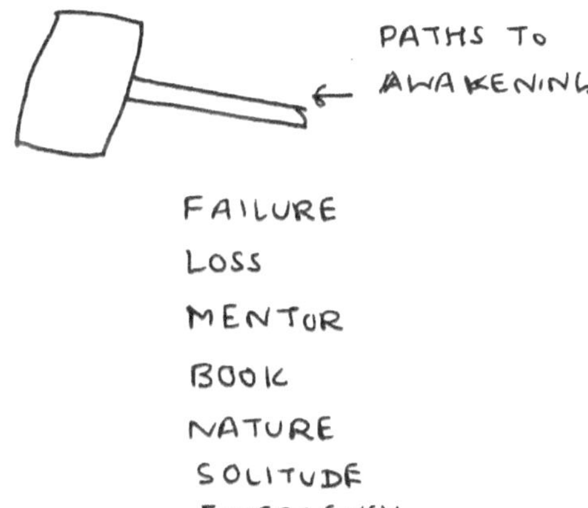


Or just with time, as your brain matures and it is exhausted of the artificial life.

It starts to wake up slowly.

This is called awakening.

The most beautiful thing a soul can feel.

It is above everything.

Beauty.

Fame.

Power.

Youth.

Then you start to awaken.

1.  To see that you are not your brain.

2.  You are not your thoughts.

3.  You are a part of infinite intelligence.

4.  You can do many things.

5.  You can control the car.

Then you try to find where you are going.

You realise that you are not a particular thing.

You were a child.

Then, a teenager.

Now an adult.

The car has changed.

It has grown.

But you are the same.

A small sphere of energy.

Sitting somewhere inside.

Watching everything.

You are energy.

You are not your ego.

You are not your body.

You are not your brain.

You are not your emotions.

You are not your past.

Now you know the real you.

You start to observe your brain.

You start to see your attitude.

You see the outside world more clearly.

# CHAPTER 18

# Purpose

*"Quietly endure, silently suffer and patiently wait."*

– Martin Luther King Jr.

Purpose.

You realise two things at this point -

1. **Life is short.**

   You and everyone and everything around you will be gone and forgotten in a few decades. It all means nothing. On a grander time scale, you are nothing.

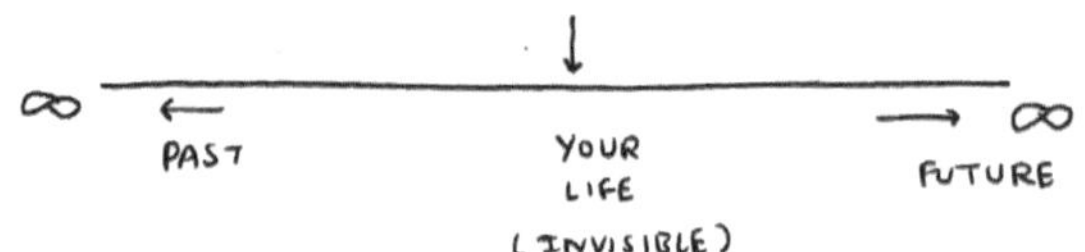


2. **And you start to crave for a purpose. Meaning of it all.**

   Where is my car going?

   What is my destination?

   What am I here for?

   What can I do?

   These questions flood you.

You feel like a person who wakes up in the middle of the day after a long sleep. Then, he is confused for some time, realising that he was in a dream, and now reality has come face to face.

According to **Sigmund Freud** the main motive propelling humans is pleasure. Great psychiatrist **Alfred Alder** concluded that the main motive is acquisition of power. But **Viktor Frankl** had to incinerate his soul in Nazi camps to realise that the main force that keeps a man going is his search for meaning.

You have external purposes.

Money. Fame. Lands. Achievements.

These all are good. Noble.

But these are usually empty when you reach them.

They are part of a hedonic pond that dries as soon as you reach it. Your throat is left dry.

You need something else to fill your soul again.

The dissatisfaction becomes permanent on that route.

Earlier, you realise that it is better to change the course.

# CHAPTER 19

# Happiness Trap

*"Limit your 'always' and your 'never'."*

– Amy Poehler

Then what is your purpose?

You ask.

Happiness?

What is happiness?

Let's assume that your purpose is to be happy.

Happiness?

It is a difficult target.

No one has seen the land of true happiness. It is not a place to reach. But it is a road which sprinkles happiness every few kilometers.

You never reach the land of eternal happiness.

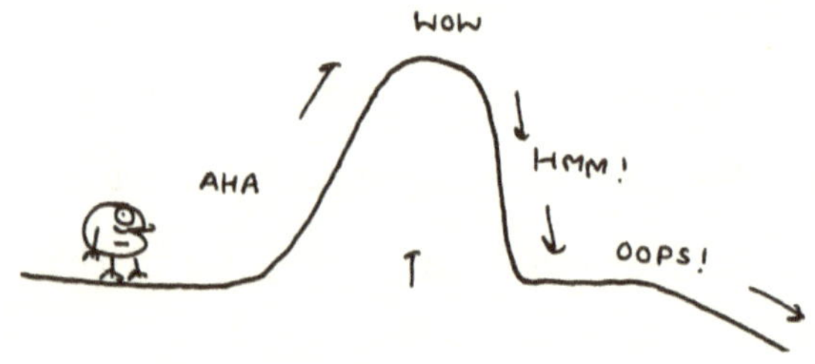

Happiness with time

First, because there is doubt if such land exists.

Second Life is too short to aim for it.

Third, even if you reach it, then it is questionable if you will like it for long.

Target **eudaimonic** happiness. It is derived from meaning and purpose in your life and by reaching your potential and by feelings of belonging. It does not depend on material things.

There is **PERMA** model of happiness. Happiness does not depend on any single thing.

Happiness depends on following five aspects of your life –

Positive emotions. (Frequency of positive emotions is more important than their intensity)

Engagement with life.

Relationships which are fulfilling and secure.

Meaning in your life and work.

Accomplishments in work and life which give you happiness.

**Savour** your life. It means to acknowledge the value of a thing and appreciate it fully.

You can savour your life by doing these things – Slow down.

Pay full attention to what you are doing.

Use all your senses.

Stretch the experience.

Reflect on it afterwards.

Best moments in life are the times when you are deeply engaged in some work which you want to do for its own sake. You will do it even if nobody pays you to do that work. This state is called state of **Flow**.

In state of flow your mind and body are stretched to their limits in a voluntary effort to do something challenging and worthwhile.

**Essential elements of a state of flow are –**

It is a challenge you can do by stretching your limits a bit.

Goals are clear and there is clear and immediate feedback.

You are in a state of deep focus.

You lose track of time.

You always feel in control of the situation.

You are completely absorbed in the task.

You are not self conscious while doing it.

You want to do this task for its own sake.

This is the state achieved by great athletes and great artists.

It happens when moderately challenging task meets a medium or highly skilled mind. If the task is very easy you get bored and if it is very difficult you feel stress.

Adversity makes happiness more desirable.

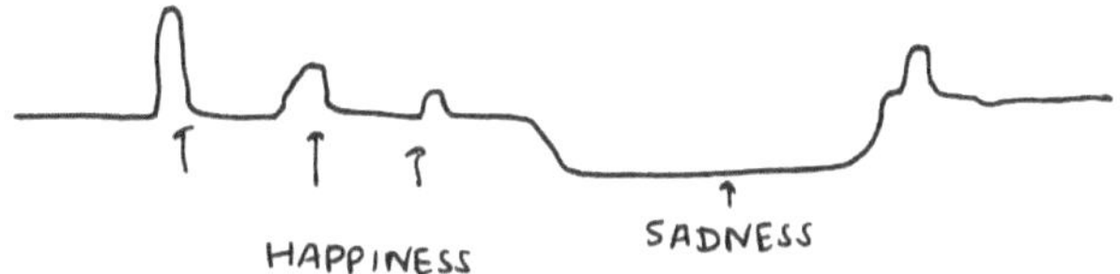


It is clear that self-happiness is not the sole purpose of your life.

You are energy, which is wise enough to realise that happiness is a choice.

You have everything now that you need. You only need to open your eyes and see.

Things you crave for are artificial. They will never fulfil you.

Happiness is your natural state of existence.

As author Rita Brown said," Happiness is pretty simple : someone to love, something to do, something to look forward to."

Then what is the purpose of the backseat traveller?

**It is to give.**

**To give back to the universe.**

To this land.

This car. (Body)

This community.

Ecosystem.

Earth.

And the universe.

To infinite intelligence.

Give back anything you can.

Reduce some entropy.

Reduce some chaos.

Serve others.

Help others reach happiness.

Take care of your car. (Your body)

Take care of the freeway. (Your environment)

Take care of other people. (Community)

That's the purpose.

It is the only purpose.

It is the purpose that every great man has ever accomplished.

Everything else is unnecessary.

Everything else is just a temporary pause.

The universe can do without them.

# CHAPTER 20

# Final Destination

*"Time moves in one direction, memory in another."*

– William Gibson

Final destination.

Then the destination arrives.

The one that you all fear.

But that's so laughable.

You were dead for eternity.

And you lived for a few decades.

Then, you will be dead for eternity.

Why do you fear?

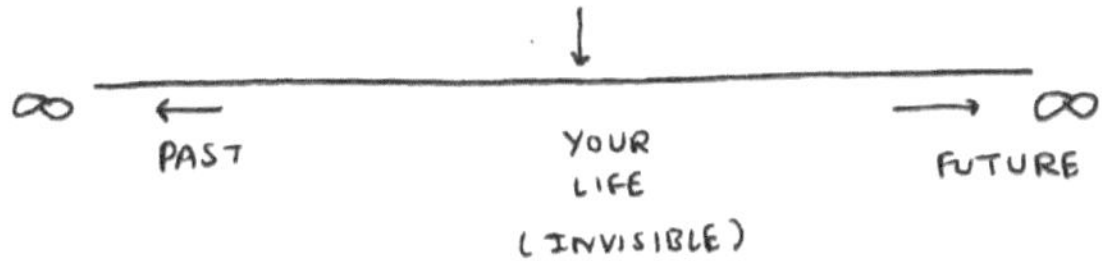



Fear of the inevitable.

Death is a certain thing.

More certain than all the things you desire.

Know this for two reasons.

You will be at peace when it arrives.

And you can enjoy this short time more if you know that you are not here for eternity.

So, our car is more certain now.

It has a purpose.

To help the universe.

To give back.

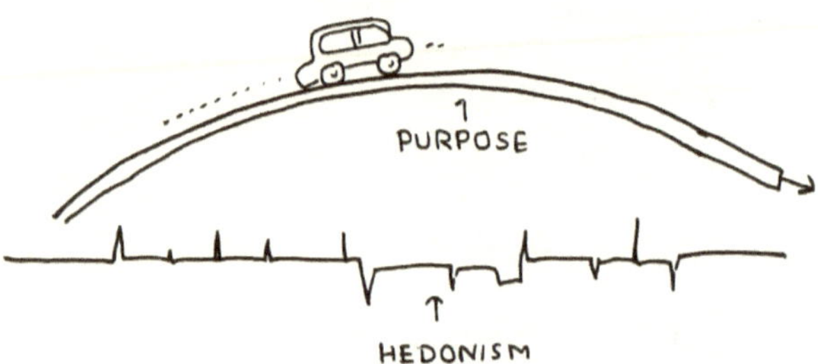

# CHAPTER 21

# How can we Give?

*"Every accomplishment starts with the decision to try."*

~ Brian Littrell

How can we give?

It is by selfless actions.

Do your work according to nature and justice.

Do what a **prudent man** will do.

Act in accordance with nature.

Without attachment to the results or fruits.

Lest you Fail.

Learn.

Change course.

Fail again.

Learn.

Improve.

And keep doing it till you have served enough people.

Instead of asking what's in it for me, ask what I can give.

Failures are the lessons given by infinite intelligence.

## What are the wrong ways to deal with failure?

Personalisation.

Thinking it as final.

Losing hope.

Catastrophising.

Self sabotage.

Guilt.

Generalisation.

Inevitability.

Excuses.

Learn to fail well. Change your relationship with failure. Failure is feedback from the universe. It is a system to improve your creation. It is a step on the ladder going to success. Failure is universal. There is no system or person which has never failed.

Everything and everyone has to fail eventually.

Take failure with a brave heart. Take it on your own shoulders.

So you can give your services to others when you are alive but what after that?

## What can you give to this world after you are dead?

First of all, why did you come into existence?

You have come here to make this universe a little better. That's clear now.

# CHAPTER 22

# What can you Give?



*"All limitations are self-imposed."*

– Oliver Wendell Holmes

What can you give?

I think there is only one thing that you can give back.

**Your thoughts.**

**Yes.**

Better thoughts.

To the coming generations.

Throughout, I have tried to detach you from your thoughts. But now I want you to give these thoughts!

Quite an irony!

But that's how the world works.

We deal through brains. We float in the consciousness. And it deals in thoughts.

What else can we give?

And brains exchange thoughts.

These are put into books or minds of the knowledge keepers.

Knowledge breeds in collective consciousness.

People who collect great ideas are pioneers.

They identify them. They learn them. Then they transfer these to their progeny.

That is the process that makes the civilisations.

Everything else is temporary. It all becomes fossil or artefacts.

Only good thoughts survive. So focus on them.

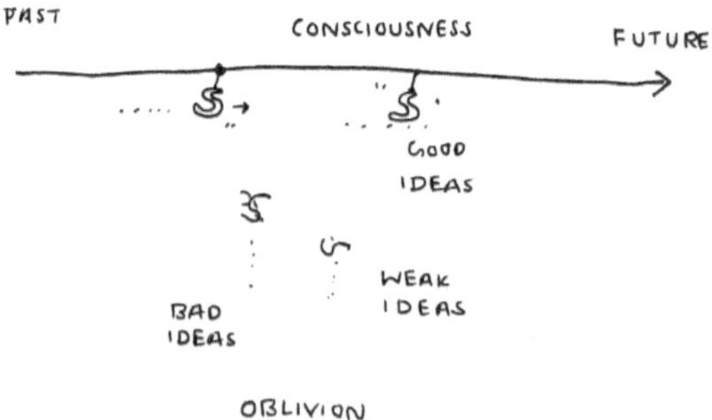


Thoughts trickle down through each generation.

Good thoughts are chosen.

They enlighten billions of brains.

These thoughts carry the message.

The information which is as vital as consciousness.

Organised thoughts create information.

Consciousness feeds on information.

It will be useless without information coming inside it. A conscious organism without thoughts will be as good as a dead one.

It interprets information through the brain and its experience.

So, thoughts are not harmful in themselves. They are necessary to make consciousness useful. These make the consciousness legible to us.

We harm ourselves by handling them badly.

You need to handle them correctly.

Good thoughts are last to fade away from the combined consciousness of civilisation. Even Gods started as an idea in the brains of our ancestors.

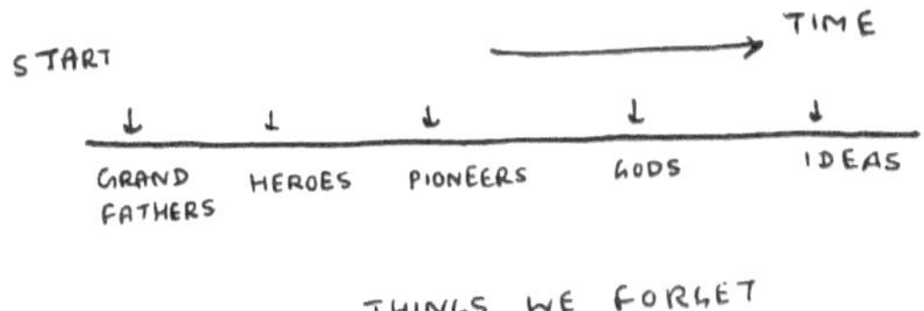


## So what about the next generations?

They are all your kids. Your descendants. You have to reach out to them through these thoughts and ideas.

Good ideas worth transmitting are specialised thoughts with intended positive output. They start as hunches and become a habit and then culture.

They spread from one brain to another. They are resilient.

They survive.

They chase consciousness.

They appear in it and change the consciousness.

Then consciousness (I mean you) either acts on it and propagates it.

Or it rejects it.

In that case, the idea becomes dormant for a long time.

After a long time, which nobody knows, it dies.

But we are not sure if it will die permanently.

Because it can rise back as waves of culture. Fashion. Laws. Traditions.

Or it can arise de novo.

At some different time.

So now, about your descendants!

It doesn't matter if they remember you.

Everyone is forgotten in enough time.

Awards don't matter.

So, many Nobel laureates. Nobody remembers the names. Even the Noble academy is perishable after a very long time.

Even kids forget their great grandfather's in decades.

Who are you then?

After death we forget ourselves.

But good thoughts should survive.

These should grow.

So, give good ideas to generations.

Templates to live according to. So that their life is worth living millions of times.

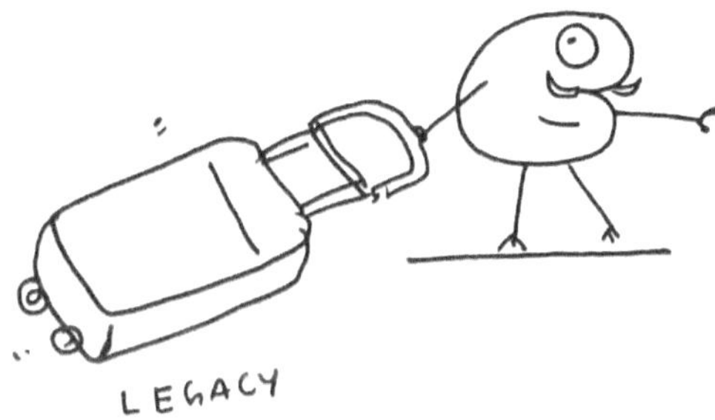


**So the summary of this all is -**

**when alive, serve others.**

**After that, at the end leave good ideas.**

Don't seek fame or immortality.

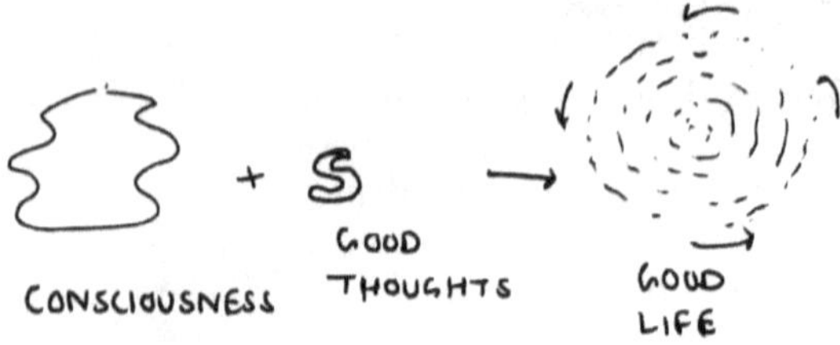


That defeats the purpose. And even if achieved it hardly matters.

# CHAPTER 23

# Dealing with Loss

*"Happiness is not by chance, but by choice."*

~ Jim Rohn

So you now know that there is only one thing worth leaving for your community.

But before that, you should learn to die well after you have lived a good life.

**How to deal with death?**

Dying of a loved one is in some ways your own death.

Pain has the similar magnitude as your own death.

How to accept the death of a close one?

Know that they will be around.

In some other form.

They are not annihilated.

They just change.

They are forms of energy like you.

They leave one car and one brain behind.

They then enter something else.

Till we work that out let's say they enter a different state of existence.

State which our consciousness cannot fathom. Part of them which you own as a result of your deep connection stays with you.

Around you.

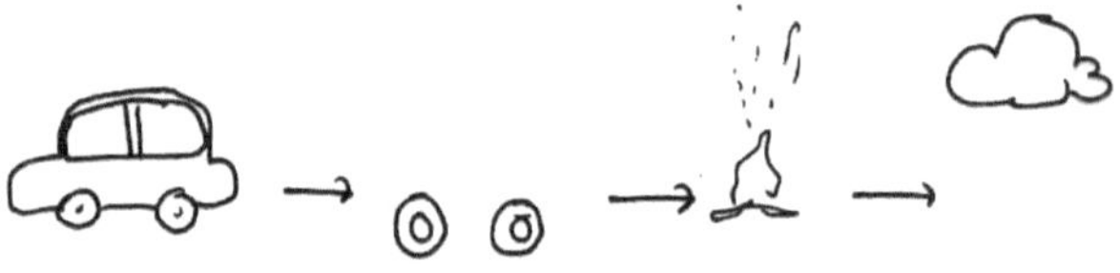



You can feel their presence every day in your own body and thoughts.

They survive as thoughts called memories.

A part of them always stays.

Other parts are transformed into other elements.

Not identifiable. But existing.

After all, everything is made up of the same stuff.

Your own death. Now the real thing. Well, it is difficult.

Prepare every day.

Remember it every day.

Face it with grace.

You don't want your kids to see the fear or agony in your eyes when you wish them goodbye.

Grow lions out of them.

Show them the path.

It is like a home to which you return after a long but useful journey.

Final resting place. Face it with dignity.

Without remorse.

Without fear.

Without shame.

Your responsibilities are endless.

You could never finish them all.

You tried hard and acted according to the nature. That is more than enough.

Your kids and everyone and the whole universe will adjust and adapt.

They will continue to survive and thrive.

Know beforehand that you can't carry anything or anyone with you. Try to become a happy memory.

And what is a memory?

Well, that's also a thought. A happy thought. A thought that gives a person power to keep going.

So, at the end of it all you meet me again.

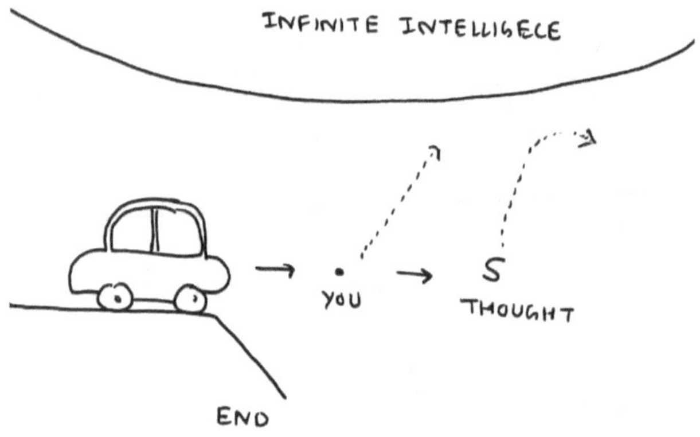


Your thoughts.

We both are immortal.

You are a soul that will return to infinite intelligence.

I am the thought that you created. I may be more immortal than you. I will return as soon as you come to consciousness.

So, I hope we will meet again inside some other car.

**Always remember you are a tiny wisp of energy (soul) carrying a big corpse.**

**– Epictetus.**

REAL
ME
MY
BRAIN
BODY   ME

# CHAPTER 24

# Satan and the Faust

Once there was a man. He was called Faustus.

When he turned 18, he became restless and started craving power, wealth, and pleasures. Then, he went to the high hills where Satan lived. He could grant any wish he had heard.

He made a trade with the Satan. He traded his soul for all the things he wanted. Although he didn't realise this at that time. His soul was necessary to feel calm and tranquillity.

"I will return after 20 years", said Satan and vanished in the cave.

Faustus enjoyed great success and wealth. He feasted on all types of pleasures.

Time passed very fast, like a gust of wind.

Finally, when he realised that his time was coming near the end, he developed the same restlessness.

Fear. Continuous irritation. Sleeplessness. All the things that he wanted to avoid. He became very sad. These were the things that he wanted to avoid. For that, he indulged his senses into temporary balms of pleasures and gluttony. But those feelings he feared were just hidden beneath his skin. They were not gone. They were there all the time.

He had been duped by the Satan. What he had traded was far more valuable than the things he got. Hence, his bargain was self-defeating.

He wanted to get rid of these things, but he had only covered them with a thin layer of indulgences.

He realised what a big mistake he had made. He should have kept his soul, which would have shown him the better path.

Whatever was required to quench his cravings was always there inside his soul.

He waited in extreme agony for the day when Satan would return to pull him into eternal hell.

Lesson - Don't trade something of supreme moral and spiritual value with worldly or material benefits.

# Part 2

# Learning the Ways to Create Good Thoughts (Most of the Time)

# CHAPTER 25

# Producing Good Thoughts – A Simple Recipe

We are all businessmen. We all are, even if you are not aware of it.

We are in the business of producing thoughts. Big, small. Good and bad.

Then we serve these to all other people.

They either accept and like them. Or they dislike these and stay away. Some people may stay neutral.

But that is the reality.

Thoughts you produce are transmitted to the universe and the quality of your thoughts decides what the universe will send back.

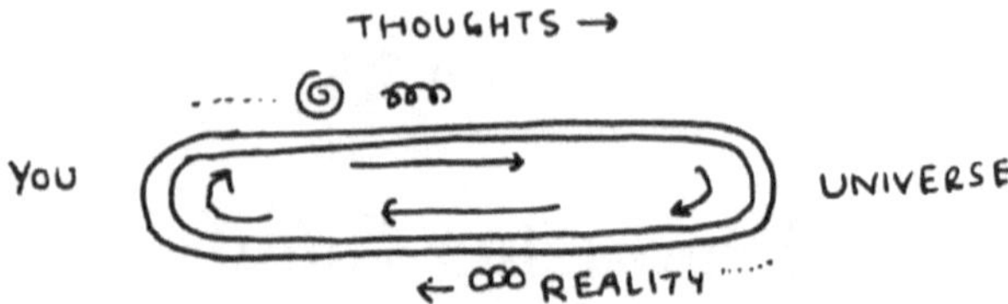


So it is a good idea to produce good thoughts. These good thoughts will create a good life for you and your community.

Let's focus on another fact. We all live inside a bubble. A bubble of **subjective reality.** Its maximum diameter is the distance which light can cover and return during our lifetime. That reflected light can be detected by our big telescopes and through that you sense the returning data. That is a huge distance.

But it is not very useful except for research in an astronomical lab.

Our practically useful subjective bubble is very small. We stay inside it most of the time. It starts just on our skin and ends on the surface of other brains with whom we interact most of the time.

A few times, it expands in size when we call someone on the phone or a dead author leaves a book read by somebody centuries later.

Expanse of our bubble stretches over distance as well as on time scale on these occasions.

Otherwise our subjective bubble extends to the margins of our immediate surroundings and our community. We exchange thoughts continuously inside it. So where we live decides a lot about the types of thoughts we create and exchange. This is called our conditioning.

Then, there is our inner universe.

If we look inside us, then there is infinite depth there, too. But generally, monks who meditate for years experience this depth.

We need to take care of this bubble.

It is our reality, and it affects every action we take.

Everyone is moving with their subjective bubble. You should not dare to change it or break it. You can only help another person to change it himself. That too is a very slow process. This bubble can be changed from inside only. External inputs only assist.

This bubble starts as a very small thing in our childhood. It includes only your mom, your milk bottle and things near your bed. Then it gradually gets filled up with all kind of thoughts.

Things filling it up are

1. Culture of the country you are born in.

2. Religious beliefs and rituals.

3. Your immediate community and teachers.

4. Written or audio information you get while you move in time.

5. Your subjective experience and interpretations.

So it is already a full bubble when you realise that you live inside it all the time. And you need to make it a nice place to be.

The good news is that this space is very flexible and can be modified by you.

Deal in good thoughts to do that. Produce good thoughts and receive good thoughts.

So let's return to our thoughts factory again.

So you are the CEO of this idea factory that is sitting on your shoulders. It is working continuously night and day.

An average human creates 60000 to 80000 thoughts per day. And these all are shipped to you and many are shipped to others.

So it is a very important job to take care of this production.

There are few basic truths that govern your factory. These govern everyone's thinking.

These are -

1. You have a choice to choose your thoughts. You can prefer one over the other.

2. Every thought has an effect, however minute it may be. Good thoughts lead to good results. Bad thoughts have bad fruits.

3. Repetition, focus, and practice make a thought stronger and live longer.

4. Like nature, you should create thoughts with a focus on the long term.

5. You have to energise good thoughts to keep them alive.

6. Humans work on incentives and drives.

7. Every action must be preceded by a thought in your brain.

8. Thoughts and their interpretation are not the same.

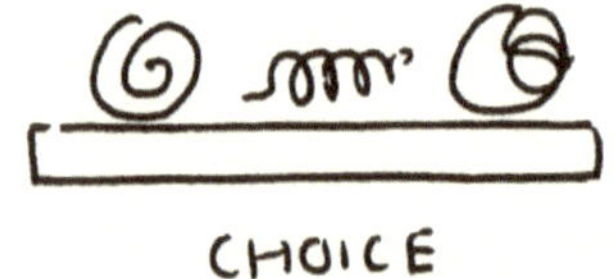

CHOICE

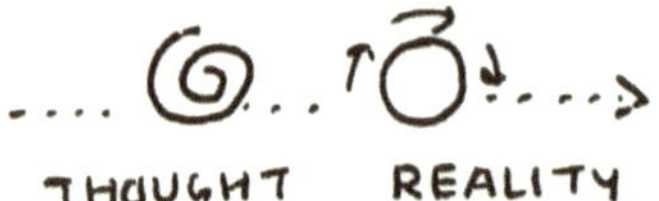

THOUGHT    REALITY

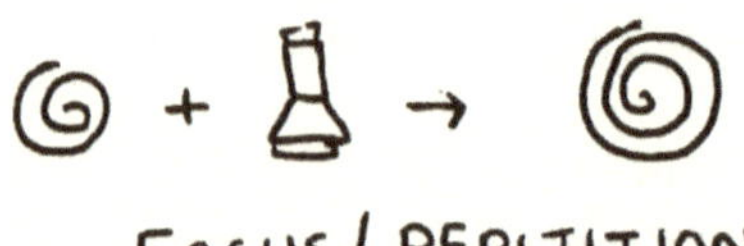

FOCUS / REPITITION

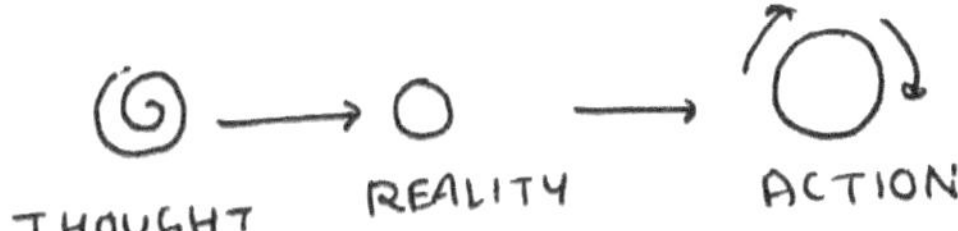


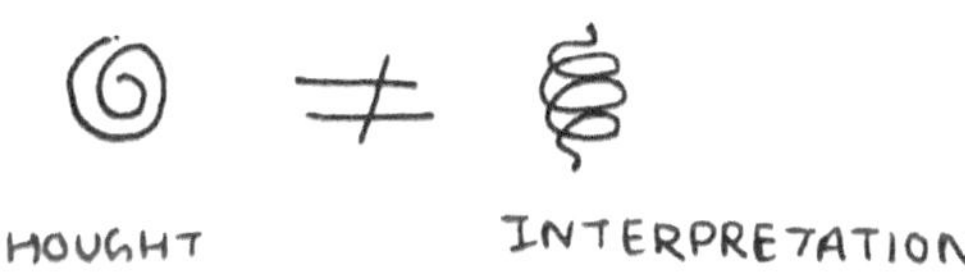


Raw material for our thoughts factory.

We start with the raw material for great thoughts.

These are your basic beliefs. These were formed by your upbringing and your surrounding influences. They serve as the mine from which new thoughts arise.

They are stored in your subconscious mind. They are stored as memories and hunches and models of thinking.

Beliefs about beliefs are called meta-beliefs. They are rocks from which raw material is extracted.

They should be healthy and good.

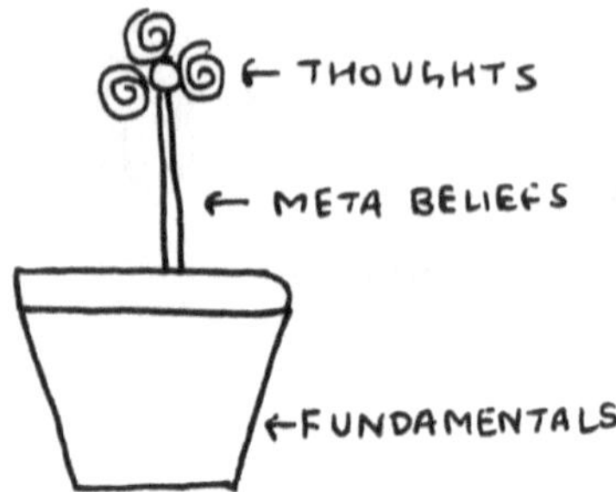


## A Few Good Meta-beliefs are -

1. Change is a constant thing.

2. Failure is a normal part of success.

3. Our thoughts shape our reality

4. We are not entitled to everything.

5. Time is the most precious thing, and it is limited.

6. Everything is possible.

7. Everything is learnable.

8. I am responsible for my life, no one else.

9. Everyone can improve with time.

10. There is enough for everyone's needs.

. . . . . . . . . . . . . .

. . . . . . . . . . . . . .

. . . . . . . . . . . . . .

They are infinite. These are only a few examples. You have to choose the right ones for yourself.

Now, when you have chosen the fundamental beliefs, it's time to plan the ways in which you are going to create great thoughts.

You need a **vision** for that and your **values**.

These guide you in the right direction and help you focus your energy on one place.

Vision is your 'Why.'

Your purpose.

Reason for the fluttering of your heart with joy when you pursue a particular thing.

Become aware of the capabilities your factory has.

**Be aware.**

Know the following things -

1. Your strengths.

2. Your weakness.

3. What matters for a good life?

4. What do you want?

5. What skills do you need to develop?

6. Where are you right now?

7. Where do you want to go?

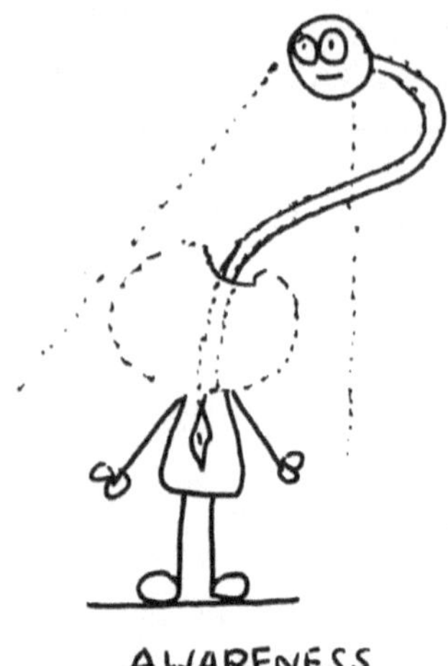



These help you in focussing your resources so that you get the maximum productivity.

Now the raw material has reached the factory. Now you need a production process. Way in which you will convert this raw material into beautiful thoughts.

First thing you need is help. All the things that can help you in creating good thoughts.

First is **clarity**. It means being clear about the reality.

This you know from your exercise when you created awareness about your life situation above. Awareness brings clarity when combined with vision and values.

Now collect a few tools.

First are **habits**. Habits are the things we do daily without much conscious effort. These cover 40-45% of our time. So good habits are a must for leading a good life.

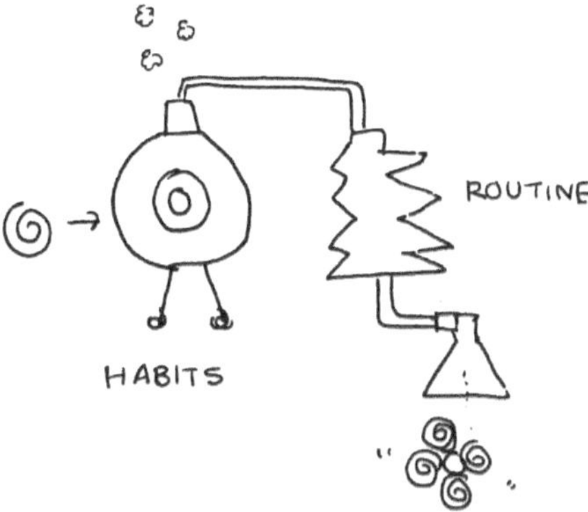


Then there are **routines**. These are similar to habits but need a little effort from our side. Most important are morning and evening routines.

If we can develop good routines for our day both at the start as well as the end, then we have a decent control on our mood and productivity.

Routines put you in right frame of mind to do the things which are priority for you.

Develop good routines.

Then there are **skills** which you need to learn.

Try to learn things which will help you be more effective in your work.

Few skills are required in every season and at all places.

These are -

Persuasion Influence

Marketing skills

Sale skills

Leadership

Creativity

Emotional intelligence

Communication skills

Prediction skills

Discipline

Learn these.

Don't cram your school and college books. Learn practical skills instead.

Now pass your thoughts through your **mental models.** These consist of your ways of seeing reality.

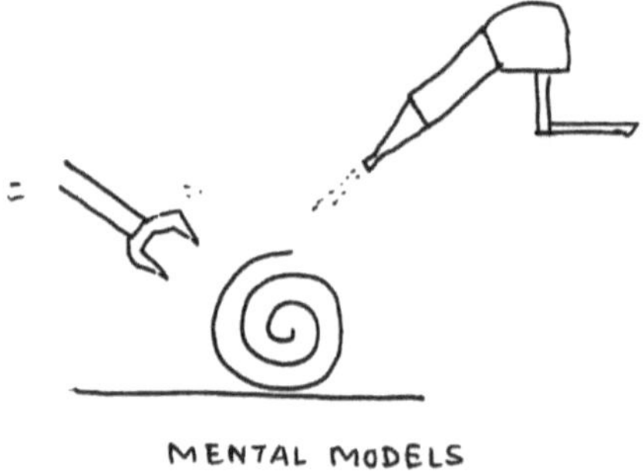


These are made slowly by your experiences and influences.

Decide your **strategy** which means group of tactics required to reach a particular goal.

**Tactic** is the specific thing which needs to be done now and it forms part of the overall strategy.

Look for any defects in the product.

Look for the **biases** which we humans commonly suffer in our thinking.

Remove biases like availability bias, hindsight bias and many other similar biases. Remove any **distortions** in the thinking.

(As you have learnt in earlier chapters)

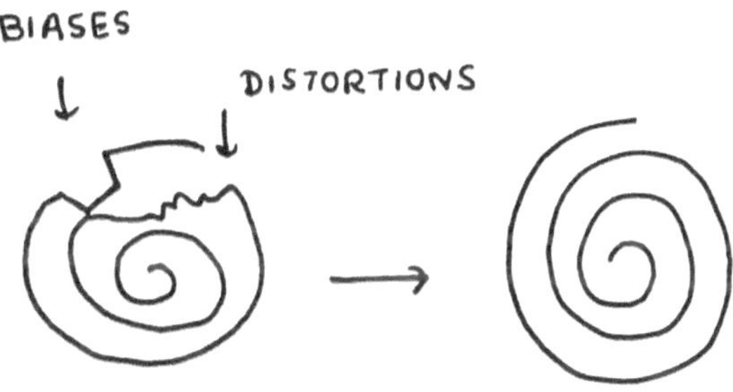


Produce your thoughts which have long term expiry. Every thought should be for your ultimate goals.

Now we have got a nice and clear thought in front of us.

Now we need to work on its **size** and **intensity**.

Make sure your thought is positive and moral.

Now make it **big**. You need to think big to succeed in your life. Make it bigger than your biggest imagination.

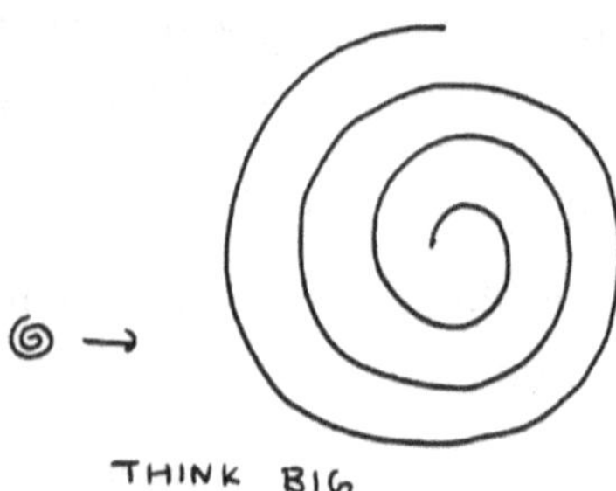


## Now Energise the Thought

This can be done by various methods.

1. First is by desire. Do things which produce deep desire and motivation in you.

2. Give attention and intention to this good thought to energise it.

3. Use visualisation techniques for your goals. See yourself as if you are already possessing the things you are striving for. Visualise yourself as already being successful. This makes your intuition and subconscious active.

4. Revisit the thought regularly either mentally or in written form so that it becomes deeply imprinted.

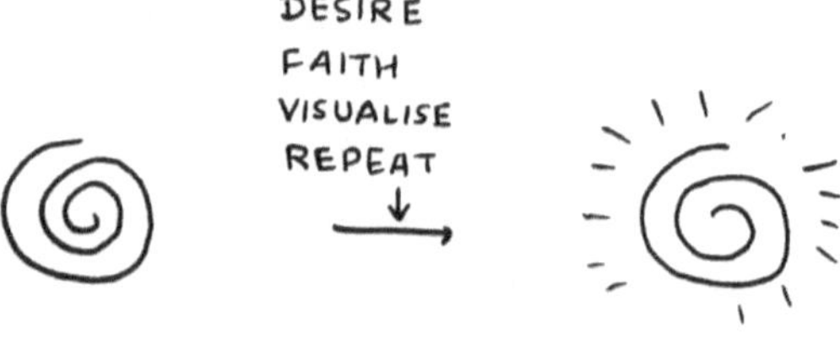

Now you have an almost ready thought which is energised by your energy.

Now use other people to polish it further.

Use **technology** like books and the internet if you need to research about it. Go to a **mentor** to give you further inputs.

Go to a friend or customer to get **feedback** about your latest production.

If thoughts are to be mass produced use money and labour of other people. Delegate work which is repetitive.

Now that is a bestsellers type of thought inside your head ready to shake the world.

But the market is ruthless. It needs things it doesn't know it doesn't need.

So to give them what is good for them is a hard work.

You will fail. No one will buy your thoughts. They will keep accumulating in your warehouse.

You will think about quitting everyday. But at that point your thoughts need you the most.

You will need **resilience** here which is the ability to bounce back from setbacks.

And grit.

**Grit** is the ability to sustain interest and effort for achieving long term goals. Worthwhile thoughts cannot survive without these.

Now your nice supple thought is ready for the user.

Pack it into nice words. Frame it in a nice frame. Ship it with words or sounds.

Then see how it creates magic for everyone.

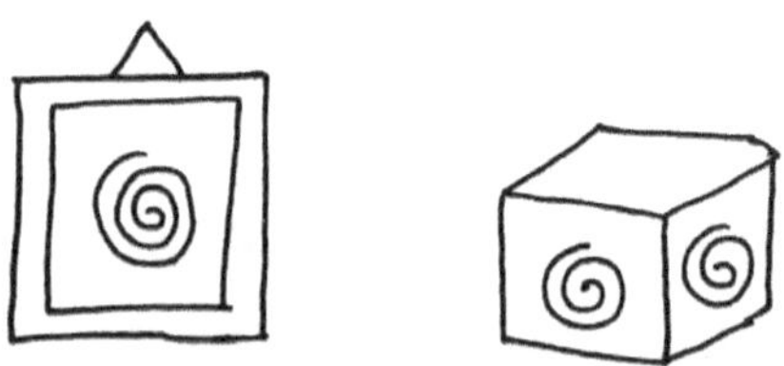

**Let's look at all this again.**

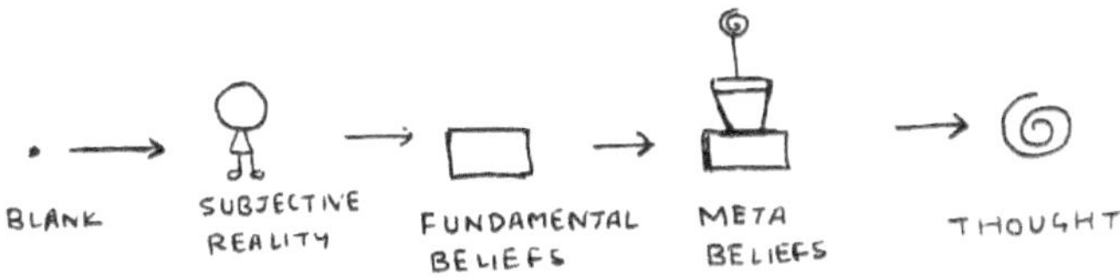
BLANK
SUBJECTIVE REALITY
FUNDAMENTAL BELIEFS
META BELIEFS
THOUGHT
BIAS
DISTORTION
MENTAL MODELS
ENERGISE
GRIT

# CHAPTER 26

# Thoughts for Videogamers

*"I have found that if you love life, life will love you back."*

– Arthur Rubinstein

And what would happen if we had to make a video game on thoughts?

**Let's see.**

**Level 1**

**See that thoughts as they arise from the underworld of the subconscious. This world that stays away from the consciousness.**

## Level 2

### Take responsibility

Learn about the whole terrain of the game. All the tools a weapons. All the mazes. All the coins to be collected.

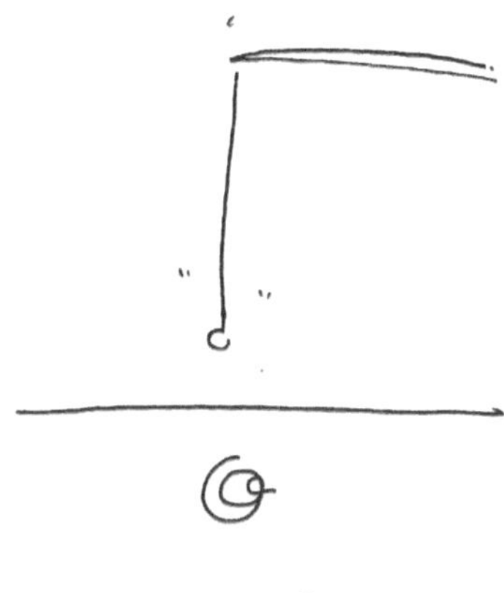



## Level 3

Be aware of all your strengths and weaknesses.

Take responsibility to end the game by killing the master demon and clearing all the stages of the game.

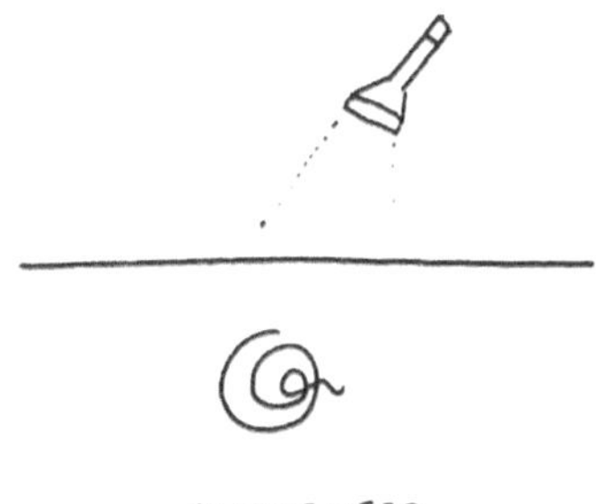

## Level 4

**Decide your avatar. Take decisions. Your weapons. Your coins. Your stars. Your shield.**

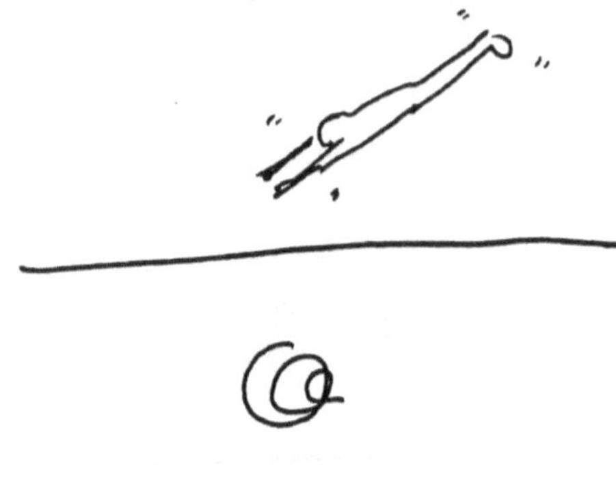



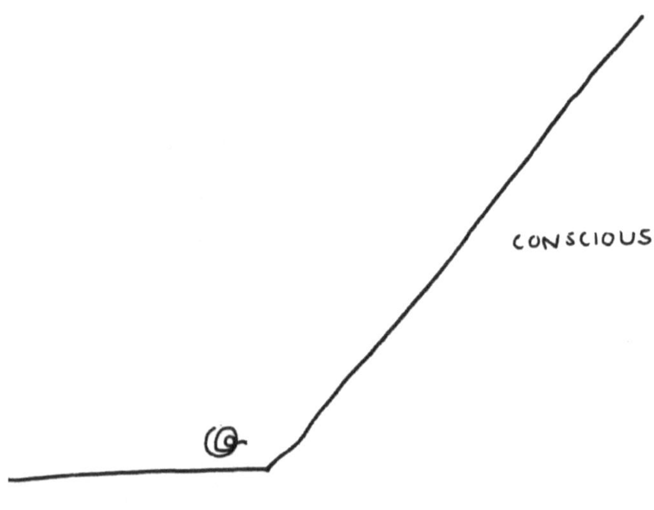

## Level 5

**Believe that you can win and clear all the levels. Have a growth mindset.**

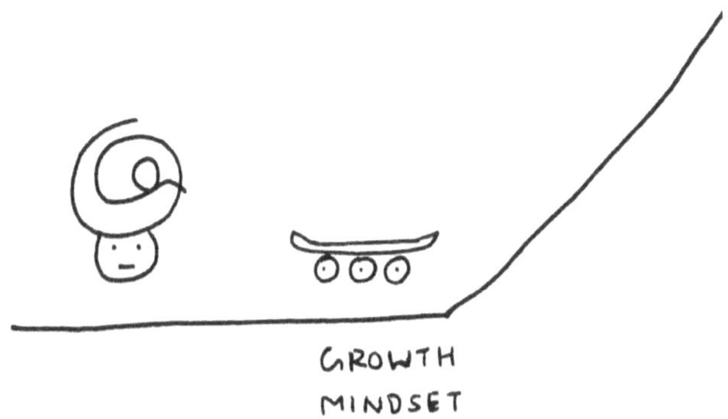



## Level 6

**Use special powers that you acquire as you play the game and kill the monsters. Use practice and repetition. Use empowering mental models.**

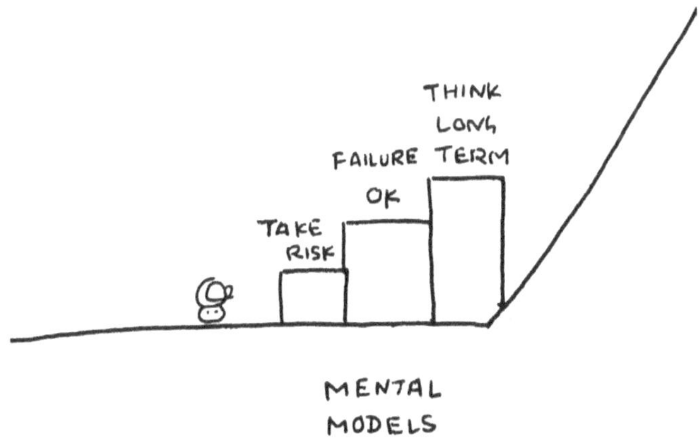

## Level 7

Use extraordinary powers that will increase your productivity and skills. Use focus. Set SMART goals. Use 80/20 principle (Pareto principle).

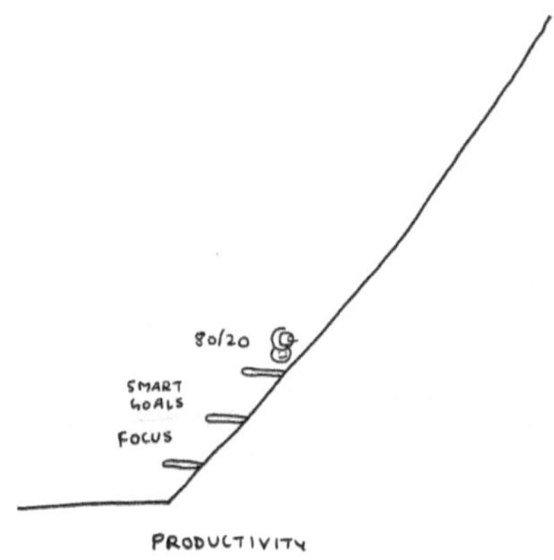



## Level 8

Collect all the stars, diamonds and emeralds available in the game. These are gratitude, forgiveness and self-compassion.

## Level 9

**Kill the dragon and reach the castle.**

**That's when you win.**

# CHAPTER 27

# The Main Thing

*"If you think you have it tough, read history books."*

– Bill Maher

Now, let's focus on the real thing. What matters the most?

Thinking is good. Thoughts are great.

You create great thoughts everyday and send them out. And you also collect great thoughts from others.

You keep them stacked in your cortex, right on the display counter of your consciousness.

But then something happens. They start to lose weight. These become shrivelled and blurry. These start to wilt away.

You go to them. Tender them and cuddle with them. You put balm on their wounds and sing heartful folk songs to heal them.

You bring ointment of your past achievements, but nothing seems to work.

Your thoughts are dying.

They are so fragile. You never realised that when you were creating them.

You are confused. What is wrong with your baby.

You go to the biggest hospital. But there is no specialist to revive them.

Then one day one wise man speaks up. He is your grandfather with a mouth full of missing teeth.

"Son, we used to work till we died in the good old times."

"Action keeps you young. Act. Do. Work. Put in the long hours. Move your muscles."

Said the grandfather who was still happy most of the time while he was wilting due to his old age.

Then you realise it.

Thoughts are thoughts only. They die without action. Act on good thoughts, and they will blossom.

Act on good thoughts. Keep them alive and healthy.

How to act to keep your good thoughts healthy and kicking?

You can call it **Daffodil principle**. It means small steps taken consistently towards your goals and improving slowly as you go. This is also called compound effect or daily continuous improvement. Using this you can move mountains. Japanese call it **Kaizen** technique. Small comfortable steps that improve with time.

If you improve 1% everyday for one year in a particular field, you will be 37 times better. It also works in the other direction. If you become 1% worse each day for one year, you will be down by 97% from initial number of 1.

So focus on consistency and gradual improvement. Although this process cannot be applied to everything and there is plateau for every skill and process.

So next time you feel stuck, it know that you might be working with daffodil principle and progress is happening but not visible to you.

# CHAPTER 28

# Beggar and the Trunk

In the street of the main market sat a beggar. Old bearded man with twisted bones. His skin lacked any trace of oil, and his eyes had lost their sheen. He begged from morning to night, from summer to winter.

One day, a wise man walked by. He gave him a few cents.

Then he asked, "Brother, what are you sitting upon?"

"Nothing," said the beggar.

"But there must be something!"

"I never checked it. I never realised. I was too busy looking for the money in the hands of my patrons."

That wise man walked away surprised.

Finally, one day, when too many wise men had passed by, each reminding him about the trunk he was sitting upon all this while.

He looked at it. A big trunk. Rusted. Dusted. No locks. He opened it. And this caused him to open his mouth in amazement.

All the real wealth of the world was already there inside that box. All the time. He was busy collecting shells from outside. But he always had access to real wealth and happiness and tranquillity with him. He was searching in the wrong places all the time.

Lesson - Everything that you need to be happy is inside you and within your reach. Open your eyes and embrace it.

# Part 3
# Perspective and its Effect on Thoughts

# CHAPTER 29

# Perspective

Perspective is a particular way of thinking about something. There are seven types of perspectives in psychology, but we are concerned with cognitive perspective only as it is linked to thinking.

Let's see our point in detail.

Suppose you are returning home after a usual soul-wrenching day at the office.

On the last turn, before you reach home and disappear behind the door, a car comes from behind at a crazy speed.

You are livid with anger. You could kill him with your hands if you could catch his car. You blurt out all the abusive stuff you have. You even consider dialling the number of your don friend who has recently come out of prison on parole.

You reach home. You kick the front door. You neglect your pet dog and your kid who have come out of pure anticipation of seeing a normal dad returning home.

You get to your bed at 1 am, still upset about that driver.

**Now, let's change the perspective.**

Imagine your thinking brain is inside your skull, but the real you are watching from a distance.

If you are sitting on the traffic light (observing from there) then you will see that two cars have interacted on a busy road. No one is harmed. Universe is working fine.

If you are sitting inside a third car as an old wise mature kind of human you will laugh at the antics of underdeveloped human beings in those two cars.

Or imagine that you later come to know that person in that car was carrying his injured son to a hospital hence he was in a hurry.

Or if you find that the car driver is your boss.

Your response to the same event will be different. Thoughts that will come out will be different. So you can see that context and your mental background changes the types of thoughts altogether.

You may even produce totally opposite thoughts.

Also, we can flip the situation. Imagine that you have recently been awarded a promotion for your work or you have just received a bonus from your company. You will not waste much time brooding on the event.

Let's stretch it further if you are sitting on the roof of a skyscraper and watching. Nothing except a few speeding metal containers.

The universe is working just fine. A cool breeze flows past you.

If you sit inside a plane, then you notice that humans have made the planet brown. There is very little greenery there, but everything still seems fine.

If you are inside a satellite sent by Elon Musk, you will see a blue ball suspended in a dark oblivion. Rotating without pauses and nourishing everyone on its surface.

If you are observing from Pluto, then you will see a big star attracting a few small lumps of silica towards it. Nothing out of the blue. No hurry in the execution.

If you ae observing from Andromeda galaxy and you could because imagination puts no limits on the absurdity of thoughts. You will see a milky galaxy moving with grace. Nobody is hurt.

And finally, it will be dark everywhere. It will be dark for all the time you could survive and observe.

Everything is the same.

So why is your world shattered by a speeding car which has not hurt you?

Change your perspective to change things.

Change perspective by doing these things:

1. Moving away from the place of an event.

2. Moving further in time by asking if this event is going to matter after five years.

3. Changing the criteria of evaluation. A thing which is bad for an individual might be perfect for the whole community.

4. See the truth behind the event. Is it an exaggerated response or an appropriate response?

5. Step into the shoes of the other person. This is called empathy.

6. Travel and interact with different cultures and people. This shows that a normal human being is not one fixed thing.

7. Get thoughts from different points in human history. That is possible by picking up great books. See how the main thinking patterns of civilisation change with time.

## Changing perspective

It is under the field of psychology. They call it cognitive behavioral therapy (CBT). This therapy tries to change your relationship with your thoughts. It is based on the belief that thoughts and emotions and actions are linked. Between a thought and action there is some gap. A small space. This is the point where you can act. It gives you power.

You can change your interpretation and hence response to these automatic and negative thoughts. You can choose a more positive and empowering interpretation. This changes your perspective.

This therapy helps you in doing all this.

Other related therapy is Acceptance and commitment therapy. This is used for things which you cannot terminate permanently. Then therapist tries to change your relationship with these. You try to peacefully coexist with these thoughts. You don't try to defeat these situations and thoughts.

Instead you try to reallocate your resources away from them. Your resources like attention, energy and time. Mindfulness and finding your true values are parts of this therapy.

# CHAPTER 30

# Empty Boat

One monk went to a monastery to learn meditation. But his monkey brain failed him for too long. In desperation, he went to a forest, but the sounds of nature bothered him.

He went to a hill, but cold winds will shake his determination. He went to a cave, but his brain remained restless.

Then, on the advice of an old monk, he borrowed a boat. He rowed it to the middle of a lake. There, he felt a few moments of calmness. He went there daily.

On day four of his meditation, he saw a boat speeding towards his boat.

"Stop," he shouted.

"Boat must belong to a pirate. some antisocial man. Amateur unable to control the boat."

He made all types of assumptions. His discomfort turned into anger, which slowly converted into fear as the other boat approached very close.

His heart raced, and his palms became sweaty, and he started to tremble with fear. He waved his hands like a madman.

Finally, the other boat reached. It struck his boat. There was a mild thud. But no real damage was done. Only the boat danced a bit. Monk saw that the boat was empty and ocean currents and winds had drifted it there. He sat there contemplating the weakness of his thoughts.

Lesson - It is always you who decides the extent of damage a particular event can do to you. Most boats that hit us are empty.

# Part 4
# Workbook

# CHAPTER 31

# That is the Correct Way to Think

*"Man suffers because he takes seriously what the Gods made for fun."*

– Alan Watts

Fundamental thoughts.

You may call them **meta thoughts.** They form the basic scaffold around which all your thoughts grow, and then they form mental models. These are models with which you scrutinise your reality.

So if your meta thoughts are positive and empowering they help you to move through reality with a graceful ease. So let's create a thought plan.

A thought is energy.

Actually, it is potential energy.

It is powerless in itself.

We provide attention and focus to it.

That way, we energise it.

With attention, focus and repetition, a thought becomes a belief.

So, if we create correct beliefs, these will show us the correct path.

**Few empowering thoughts that act as a magnet for good thoughts.**

1. Everything is learnable.

2. I can always improve.

3. I can work things out.

4. The process is the main thing. Goals will follow.

5. Persistence is a superpower.

6. I am here to make a positive change.

7. Nature has an abundance of resources for everyone.

8. I will never lose focus on my core values.

9. My core values are aligned with nature.

10. Change is the only certain thing.

**After our meta thoughts are established, we then focus on our new thoughts.**

While choosing new thoughts, keep this in mind.

1. Thoughts should be **empowering**. At no stage, give away your power to your thinking brain.

2. Thoughts should be **big.** The size of your thoughts decides the level of your success. All limitations are mind-created. You need to think beyond illusory boundaries.

3. Thoughts should be **positive**. They should harm no one. Both living and nonliving things are included. These should be aligned with the principles of justice, equity and good conscience.

4. They should be free from mental **distortions**, as discussed in earlier parts, and thinking biases.

**After the meta thoughts and new thoughts. We need to nurture these thoughts.**

**It can be done by these methods.**

1. Consume positive content

2. Switch off negative media like TV and news. Read great books. Learn from successful people.

3. Seek a good mentor in your field.

4. Take good courses.

5. Sit in the company of elders.

6. Use affirmations.

7. Routines for every important part of the day. Good routines for morning, bedtime and before your work. A good routine is half the victory.

8. Good habits. Habits are automatic routines that need little effort. They occupy 40% of our time. So try to develop good habits.

9. Fail, learn, adjust and improve.

**To do all these, we need to focus.**

**Without focus, results will not come.**

# For Focus, we need to do the following Things.

1. Be aware of your goals.

2. Write SMART goals.

3. Manage your time.

4. Reduce distractions.

5. Do one thing daily that moves you towards your goal.

6. Persist till the power of slow compounding starts acting in your life.

Thus, after some time, these things will convert your beliefs into habits, which will result in actions.

SMARTER goals -

Specific, measurable, achievable, realistic and time-bound, ethical and rewarding.

# CHAPTER 32

# Wrong Ways to Think

*"Only true wisdom is knowing that you know nothing."*

– Socrates

There are a few ways of thinking that harm us in the long term. You should be aware of them and should be ready to change them into the empowering thoughts discussed above.

1. I am entitled to everything I desire, and the universe is under obligation to serve me.

2. The universe is fair.

3. Everything, including living and non-living, should work precisely the way I want them to work so that I may feel happiness. Otherwise, I will develop negative emotions and walls against them.

4. I am born talented, and success will seek me out.

5. I can work half and succeed double.

6. There is a shortcut or hack for everything.

7. I am lucky, so I need not to worry.

8.  Everything that happens to me is due to something outside or someone else.

9.  Failure means I am not enough or worthy.

10.  I will be happy after a particular thing happens.

These are just a few examples.

Try to stay clear of these types of thoughts.

# CHAPTER 33

# A Man you Should know About

His brother was closest to him. His mother left him when he was ten years old and father lost his legal guardianship to a relative. He was perceived as not being a very bright student by his teachers.

He was trained from an early age but thoughts didn't enter easily into his simple mind. Still he learnt to speak confident English in just six months.

He was taken to distant valley of Ojai in California with his brother. He learnt yoga from Iyengar guru and visited India frequently from his adopted land. He even appeared in TV series, The adventures of young Indiana Jones, at the age of 12 years

At the age of 27 years his brother who was closest and the only link to his family and motherland, died due to chest infection. This was a big shock for his mental capacities.

His outlook towards life and depth of his perception changed. There was no hint of outward grief but he was broken from inside and changed completely. This was followed by enlightenment which usually accompanies great misfortune.

He was going to become world teacher in his religious trust but he took his own path.

He worked on teaching general public about thoughts, true freedom and truth.

He said repeatedly in his talks that truth is a pathless concept.

"You cannot organise truth into sects or religions or philosophies. The moment you follow someone, you cease to follow the truth."

He called his orations – "teachings."

He wanted to make people free from all types of mental cages and fears.

He claimed that no one was his successor and death of his body will end his awakening.

But one can touch him by living his life according to what he called teachings.

He died at the age of 91 due to pancreatic cancer. His mind was sharp till his last breath and his ashes were divided between India, England and Ojai valley, where he lived.

You can learn about thoughts by reading him and by listening to his lectures.

**J D Krishnamurti** lives on with his great legacy in form of thoughts that he has left for humanity.

# Journal for Thinking Correctly

How often do you watch your thinking brain?

..............................................................

What do you do when you have the following emotions?

Anger

..............................................................

..............................................................

..............................................................

..............................................................

Sadness

..............................................................

..............................................................

..............................................................

..............................................................

Happiness

..............................................................

..............................................................

................................................................

................................................................

## Grief

................................................................

................................................................

................................................................

................................................................

## How do these emotions change with the passage of time?

................................................................

................................................................

................................................................

................................................................

................................................................

................................................................

................................................................

## What is a better way to deal with these emotions?

## Anger

................................................................

................................................................

## Sadness

## Grief

## What are the various distortions of thought you know?

## What are the various useful ways to face fear and anxiety?

**What are the various empowering beliefs that you have?**

# What are the various wrong ways to think that has affected your life?

## How to forgive anyone in a correct way?

## How will you practice gratitude?

......................................................................

......................................................................

......................................................................

......................................................................

......................................................................

......................................................................

## Which Stoic principles can help us to lead a happy life?

......................................................................

......................................................................

......................................................................

......................................................................

......................................................................

......................................................................

......................................................................

......................................................................

......................................................................

......................................................................

......................................................................

......................................................................

......................................................................

## What are your long-term goals in life?

. . . . . . . . . . . . . . . . . . . . . . . . . . . . . . . . . . . . . . . . . . . . . . . . . . . .

. . . . . . . . . . . . . . . . . . . . . . . . . . . . . . . . . . . . . . . . . . . . . . . . . . . .

. . . . . . . . . . . . . . . . . . . . . . . . . . . . . . . . . . . . . . . . . . . . . . . . . . . .

. . . . . . . . . . . . . . . . . . . . . . . . . . . . . . . . . . . . . . . . . . . . . . . . . . . .

. . . . . . . . . . . . . . . . . . . . . . . . . . . . . . . . . . . . . . . . . . . . . . . . . . . .

. . . . . . . . . . . . . . . . . . . . . . . . . . . . . . . . . . . . . . . . . . . . . . . . . . . .

. . . . . . . . . . . . . . . . . . . . . . . . . . . . . . . . . . . . . . . . . . . . . . . . . . . .

. . . . . . . . . . . . . . . . . . . . . . . . . . . . . . . . . . . . . . . . . . . . . . . . . . . .

. . . . . . . . . . . . . . . . . . . . . . . . . . . . . . . . . . . . . . . . . . . . . . . . . . . .

. . . . . . . . . . . . . . . . . . . . . . . . . . . . . . . . . . . . . . . . . . . . . . . . . . . .

## What things do you want to do before you die?
## (Five most important things)

. . . . . . . . . . . . . . . . . . . . . . . . . . . . . . . . . . . . . . . . . . . . . . . . . . . .

. . . . . . . . . . . . . . . . . . . . . . . . . . . . . . . . . . . . . . . . . . . . . . . . . . . .

. . . . . . . . . . . . . . . . . . . . . . . . . . . . . . . . . . . . . . . . . . . . . . . . . . . .

. . . . . . . . . . . . . . . . . . . . . . . . . . . . . . . . . . . . . . . . . . . . . . . . . . . .

. . . . . . . . . . . . . . . . . . . . . . . . . . . . . . . . . . . . . . . . . . . . . . . . . . . .

. . . . . . . . . . . . . . . . . . . . . . . . . . . . . . . . . . . . . . . . . . . . . . . . . . . .

. . . . . . . . . . . . . . . . . . . . . . . . . . . . . . . . . . . . . . . . . . . . . . . . . . . .

. . . . . . . . . . . . . . . . . . . . . . . . . . . . . . . . . . . . . . . . . . . . . . . . . . . .

What would you be doing if you had all the money you need for your whole life?

....................................................................

....................................................................

....................................................................

....................................................................

....................................................................

....................................................................

....................................................................

....................................................................

....................................................................

....................................................................

....................................................................

....................................................................

....................................................................

....................................................................

## What are the things that make you really, really happy in the long term?

....................................................................

....................................................................

....................................................................

....................................................................

....................................................................

What are the various things about our thoughts that you learned from the book?

# Books to Read

*"Think yourself as dead. You have lived your life. Now take what is left and live it properly."*

— Marcus Aurelius

Shri Bhagvad Gita

The power of now

The untethered soul

Meditations

Books by Om Swami

Awaken the Giant Within by Tonny Robbins

Books by Tich Nhat Hahn

Art of Thinking Clearly by Rolf Dobelli

Thinking fast and slow by Daniel Kahneman

Mindset by Carol Dweck

Barking down the wrong tree by Eric Barker

Breath by James Nestor

Books by JD Krishnamurti

The last lecture by Randy Pausch

The happiest man on earth by Eddie Jaku

Books by Wayne Dyer

Books by Swami Vivekananda

# End of this Enchiridion

Enchiridion is a Greek word. This means a small book that contains essential knowledge about a particular subject. This is our enchiridion (handbook) about our thoughts.

It is a starting line from where you can begin your journey. It doesn't contain everything you need to know but it is a small introduction.

It is a starting point for you, but it is the endpoint of our conversation.

So here we are. Right at the end. The place which always brings both joy and tears.

Joy of being finally able to end an effort to move towards reality and sadness of still being far away.

But this is a valiant start. If you are already aware of these principles, then it is time to throw them in your routine life and fuse with them.

And if you are fresh and energetic human coming face to face with real life, then these will be valuable tools in your hands.

Don't put it away and forget it. Hand it over to the kid you know who has bright eyes and hunger for knowledge.

Few quotes to end the book on a good note.

*"You don't own anything. You are given everything for some time to keep."*

*"You are not what you own."*

*"Act according to mother nature."*

*"You can only keep what you give."*

*"You cannot change the direction of winds but you can adjust your sail."*

# Request for a Review

Friend,

If you saw few glimpses of your own thinking process in this book PLEASE leave a feedback on my AMAZON PAGE.

THANKS
Amit ☺

You can find me here -

Instagram - @bookvenger_44

Beehiiv Sunday illustrated newsletter - 100 great books as illustrated book lessons.

Email - bookvenger44@gmail.com

# About the Author

The author is a middle-aged Indian doctor who has been searching for reality all this while. He has an addiction to reading. This takes him to many dead people who were brilliant and who have left books for us. He reads and re-reads these great books. He likes to take simple notes for his simple mind. These are for his three kids, who have stacks of books piled-up in their house to nudge them towards a reading habit. He hopes that someday, young kids all over the world will read his book and know that there are infinite ways to look at reality. They have to choose the correct way for themselves.

# Epilogue

*"We suffer more in imagination than in reality."*

– Seneca

The good news is that the medical representative who had sparked the creation of this book bounced back from the disaster that life had thrown.

He joined a more humane pharma company and started to prosper once again.

**This much grit rests inside each one of us.**